Where the Action Is

MODERN STORIES AND PRAYERS

Published in co-operation with the
Christian Book Promotion Trust

COLLINS
FONTANA BOOKS

First published in Fontana Books 1972
Second Impression June 1973

© 1972 Rita F. Snowden

Printed in Great Britain
Collins Clear-Type Press
London and Glasgow

WHERE THE ACTION IS

Rita F. Snowden—apart from her books—is widely known in many countries. After six years at business, she trained as a deaconess of the New Zealand Methodist Church. She served in turn two pioneer country areas and moved to the largest city for some years of social work during an economic depression. While bedridden with a severe heart condition, she wrote her first book, *Through Open Windows*.

Her extensive travels include five years touring New Zealand, lecturing and introducing books. In Australia she was guest speaker at the Methodist Centenary in Queensland and, some years later, at the Methodist Home Mission Centenary in New South Wales; in a similar working capacity she visited other Australian states including the primitive Inland. She has also travelled widely in Europe, Palestine, the Middle East and Japan.

Miss Snowden has served the world Church—beyond the ministry of her own denomination—with regular broadcasting commitments. She has written and spoken in Britain, Canada and the United States, and in Tonga at the invitation of Queen Salote. She has represented her Church at the World Methodist Conference in Oxford, later being elected the first woman vice-president of the New Zealand Methodist Church, and president of its Deaconess Association. She is an hon. vice-president of the New Zealand Women Writers' Society, a Fellow of The International Institute of Arts and Letters and a member of P.E.N. A regular contributor to the *British Weekly* and other periodicals in the English-speaking world, she is the author of more than forty books for adults and children—three of the most recent being her anthology, *People are People* and the companion volumes: *A Woman's Book of Prayers* and *Prayers for the Family*.

CONTENTS

INTRODUCTION

I have headed this page with one word; but the whole of this little book is introduction. Always this carries some risk—'Mary meet Richard'; 'Ann meet Dr Robert'—you mightn't take to each other. But always there is the chance that it will turn out to be one of the most exciting, enriching experiences—and life never the same again.

It was that way, of course, just off the sunny glare of the street called Straight, when a certain strong character entered the cool shade of the house of Ananias—to an introduction and two wonderful words: 'Brother Saul!'

That was away back in the first Christian century, but these to whom I would introduce you are of our own vital century, the twentieth. They stand, singled out from many nations, many denominations. Of some, others have written; but not all—there hasn't been time, for they are at this moment 'where the action is'.

Like many effective introductions, these are brief—they seem best that way. One can never tell all: that belongs to the adventure we are set upon. And there is no saying where it can begin: curled up in your favourite seat; standing in school assembly; listening in your week-time club; or at the opening of your women's meeting, hushed in devotions.

This is the beauty of an introduction.

R.F.S.

THE STORY BEHIND THE STORY

Cinema patrons, or mere passers-by casting a second's glance at the bright posters, none of us can have missed knowing that *Tora! Tora! Tora!* is crammed with action. But how many of us know the story behind the story? In human values, it's a story as dramatic as that which the film sets out to show—the surprise attack on Pearl Harbour! Servicemen, statesmen, and historians now accept 7 December 1941 as one of the most significant days of World War II.

The film takes its title from words radioed by the leader of the Japanese squadron to signal that a surprise attack had been achieved: '*tora! tora! tora!*'—tiger, tiger, tiger.

Adding greatly to the interest, and to the complex task of making the film, the fateful unrolling of that happening is told from two points of view—that of the Japanese, and that of the American. At an agreed time, the two films were edited to make one. I want only to tell the story behind the story.

When the film was given its première in London, a Presbyterian minister was present, by special arrangement to view it. He might not have been the only one in the audience there for relaxation or instruction.

But there was something very special about *this* Presbyterian minister—he was Japanese! Added to that, his name was Mitsuo Fuchida. He had been the Japanese airman chosen to lead the 7 December 1941 raid on Pearl Harbour. But much had happened meanwhile. In an interview, he told of his spiritual pilgrimage. It had led him, in turn, through Shintoism, Buddhism and Emperor worship, to Christianity.

On a journey to Tokyo in 1949 to meet General Mac-Arthur, it happened that he was given a slim booklet. It bore the title *I was a Prisoner of Japan*. It told, he soon discovered, the story of Jacob de Shazer, an American captured during special missions behind the Japanese lines, and held. It was while in prison that Jacob de Shazer was given a Bible. Reading it there, he was confronted with the shining power and mastery of Christ— and became a Christian. It was a crisis experience for the young American who had systematically hated and fought the Japanese. But it was no passing whim. At last, when war was over—and preparation for his new personal adventure—he returned as a Christian missionary to live among the very people who had imprisoned him.

And it was the straightforward telling of this in the booklet which so profoundly affected ex-Commander Fuchida, and in turn set him to reading the Bible carefully. 'One month later', he was moved to say, 'I read in Luke's Gospel, the words, "Father, forgive them for they know not what they do." No one helped me to understand it. The Holy Spirit alone made it plain.'

Since then, the Japanese hero, Mitsuo Fuchida, has dedicated his life to the service of the living Christ—as an ordained itinerant Presbyterian minister visiting towns and villages.

This is 'the story behind the story'—a place where the action is!

MY PRAYER

Almighty God, I see that you are at work in the world today, in lives high and low. But there is often, I admit, a gap between what I find myself doing, and what you want me to do. This becomes uncomfortably clear at times:

through everyday happenings;
through the words in my Bible;
through the actions of others I hear of.

All too often, my need is not to be shown my way, but to find courage to walk in it. Amid the complex interests of each day, let me seek first your holy truth, and love it; your holy will, and do it. Let my devotion command all my faculties.

Where there is friction, help me to bring the cool balm of understanding; where there is insecurity, sweet confidence. Let me never be so engrossed that I do not care for my fellows.

These great things I ask, in the name of Jesus Christ, my Lord. A M E N

OUR PRAYER TOGETHER
Eternal God, in the midst of mechanical marvels, it is easy to forget that always men and women matter most; amidst noisy modern machines of industry and war, to miss your 'still small voice'. Your will for us is life— in its most glorious sense. Forgive us that ever we have given our best energies to programmes of destruction.

Forgive us that we have filled our lives with the fruits of technology, only to serve national pride and superiority.

Forgive us that we have risen early, eaten well, and gone forth clothed, forgetful of the basic needs of so many of our fellow men and women.

Forgive us that in this exciting age of outer space, we have missed so often your essential gift of inner peace.

We seek your blessing on all who stand at the crossroads of choice today—young people learning new lessons, middle-aged weary in their sustained responsibilities, old and frail grown tired in the way. We are all your earth-children. For every past experience of your love, of your guidance, of your sustaining strength, we bring in this silence our wondering praise. A M E N

WITHOUT A HALO

If there is anyone 'where the action is' today deserving of a halo, it's Winifred Coate. But the nearest she came to it, I saw, as I walked with her under the fierce Jordanian sun at Zerka, was a crown of silvery hair. At the end of thirty-nine years with young people, she had dropped retirement's attractions to help Arab refugees.

All about us, little children played happily, whilst their mothers busied themselves in the square houses she had built. Men, busy with tilling, with pottery, with breeding and tending a dairy-herd, belonged to the same white homes. And all around, green things grew that never grew in that part before. Those sharing the new life with Miss Coate would gladly have given her a halo, if it could have helped in any way one so practical.

A sizable number—looking on as early as the hot days of February 1961—would offer this softly-spoken English-woman nothing but the laughter of scorn. Fancy investing money at her age—or at any other, for that matter—in a trackless wilderness of sand and stones! About three hundred and sixty acres, fourteen miles north-east of Zerka, within reasonable distance of Amman! They knew what lived there. Nothing! Not a blade of grass, not a bird, nor any living creature, save an occasional jerboa (a desert rat that passing Bedouin might catch and eat).

The critics called the whole project 'Coate's Folly'. It looked like it. But this gentle Anglican Christian had a dream. A water-diviner with a modest twig must surely find water. Centuries had passed, but *once* Crusader castles stood thereabouts—though every least sign of habitation had now been scattered to the winds. Everybody counted it a waterless waste—everybody except Winifred Coate. The authorities refused to do a thing.

To her pleading, the Save the Children Fund leaders promised some help with the first homes, *if* water could be found. If? There was no pretending otherwise, water and life stood eternally tied. So the dreamer engaged Abu Nakhleh to walk patiently up and down over that part of the hot earth's surface with his little twig. Day after day went by. He was joined in time by four other helpers to do other tasks—carrying out from Zerka each day needful water for themselves. With pick-axes and shovels stones were cleared, roads marked, and dry walls built. A tiny building was raised—paid for by Christian Aid—a shelter for workers by day and, by night, for two watchmen keeping guard over their few tools. A folly?

Day after hot day, Abu Nakhleh walked up and down. Till suddenly his little twig resisted—resisted after so long! There *was* water! A test well proved it; Oxfam provided funds. And in no time people from miles around, who knew desperate need, were flocking to see a miracle! Pure, sweet water gushing up out of the ground!

Other wells were sunk. Men, long dispirited, seeking work, dug, carted stones, designed irrigation channels—and *planted, planted, planted*! Houses followed, and in a short time the first families were settled. Soon they had food to eat, to *sell*—peppers, lentils, cucumbers, lettuce, celery! Lush clover, and alfalfa! King Hussein paid the settlement a visit, and named the glad venture *Abdelliyeh*. And, amazed, the Government made a gift of additional desert.

A dream? Yes! But a dream realized, and today spelling life for dispirited people—thanks to a silver-haired dreamer!

MY PRAYER

O God of life, such perseverance in the service of others in desperate straits seems to me miraculous!
Such courage to complete a stubborn plan—against

ridicule, physical tiredness, and lack of funds—
makes me humble!

I seek your blessing just now on all persons and societies
everywhere, set to help men and women—especially
the dispossessed, the war-wracked, the unskilled.

I rejoice in the compassionate action of your Church
all over the earth—wherever human need presses
hard. Once, men thought to serve and glorify you
chiefly locked up within a consecrated building—
but not now.

In Christ's name, let me also take a share in the excitement of your service in this modern world in which
I find myself. AMEN

OUR PRAYER TOGETHER

O God, we bless you for all writers and speakers who
enlarge our knowledge and concern—

Give us today a lively sense of responsibility for all
burdened by want, by hopelessness:

Along with the words of our mouths, accept our material
resources, and our skills.

And bless today all who help to fashion our world's
thought—

those who direct our agricultural schemes;

those who prepare our newspapers;

those who present our films and plays;

those who speak through our radio and TV;

those who set the mood of our leisure hours;

those who in any way, bring the gospel of Christ
close to our daily need.

Give us clear eyes, steady nerves and generous hearts
this day. AMEN

AN OLD PILL BOX

It might have been tossed into the back of the fire, or put out with the rubbish. But that empty Beecham's pill box, made of a slither of wood, was still around. And so began one of the most striking success-stories of Australian Christianity. When most little fellows of seven were scuffling about outside, or inside begging for 'something to eat', little Vernon Turner was busy with that old box. He had filled it—not with pills of his own making—with a spoonful of carbon granules. Next, he had inserted two wires, and covered it with a piece of microphone to form a diaphragm.

In that small boy was lodged by God a genius for pulling things to pieces and putting them together in a new way. He had managed to buy old telephones for a few paltry shillings from P.M.G. disposals in Adelaide. And, though he was only seven, young Vernon had a clear idea of what he was doing. And that old pill box worked.

Soon, rumours got around of a more elaborate radio set, with two crystals, six coils and a dozen knobs, operating from an attic room in Glenelg. His was the uncanny job of receiving, now, stations from afar, through his head-phones. It didn't surprise any who knew Vernon that he had set his heart on becoming an electrical engineer.

But at eighteen years of age, surprisingly, God called this gadget-minded young man into the Christian ministry! It looked to most as if his wireless days were over when he entered Moore Theological College in Sydney to train for the Anglican priesthood. Fortunately, he came under the friendly guidance of wise old Archdeacon T. C. Hammond. One of his student tasks was to take his turn in standing beneath a window and delivering—with clear voice developed in his youthful 'studio' announcing to a non-existent audience—a personal cue to 'rise and shine'. 'Good morning, sir! It is six o'clock and a beautiful day, sir!'

Appointed a catechist in a parish of five churches, whilst still at Moore College, the young man gained valuable experience; and gained, too, in 1941, his life-partner—one of a number of young folk who responded to the call of Christ, through his youthful ministry.

Succeeding years led from parish to parish—with three of them out-back with the Bush Missionary Society. Strenuous years they proved—formative years, leading Vernon Turner's steps eventually into Emmanuel College, Brisbane, for further studies; followed by his ordination into the Presbyterian Church of Australia.

However many people in the 2.9 million homes from coast to coast in Australia today go to Church, ninety-seven per cent of all of those homes have radio sets and more than half of them more than one set. And God has matched this tremendous fact with another, no less modern in every way—the tested dedication and technical skill of a Christian minister (the one-time little boy who had twiddled with a home-made microphone), his wife and family and highly qualified staff of twenty. From three electronically equipped studios, the gospel of the Kingdom reaches out now to countless lives, through Sydney-based C.B.A. (Christian Broadcasting Association). Every week more than five hundred programmes are sent out to over a hundred broadcasting stations throughout the country. 'Without the C.B.A.,' the President of the Federation of Australian Commercial Broadcasters has said, 'meaningful religious programming on radio in this country would cease almost overnight.' After twenty years of this ministry, C.B.A. sees itself as a servant of the churches. The Primate of Australia's words are up to date: 'It is good to know that God has so blessed the work of C.B.A.'

More than bulging files of letters—humbly and wonderingly read in the studios—all over the land are lives

made new by the mercy of Christ. And it all started with
an old pill box and an enthusiastic small boy!

MY PRAYER

O God, I marvel at the number of ways you have of
answering our prayers—of showing us your loving care,
of enriching our lives, of leading us one by one into
relationship with yourself.

I thank you especially just now for the eager curiosity
of youth;
for the encouragement of the family;
for inventors who have spelled out in my day the
lively joys of communication.

I thank you for allowing me to live in this wonderful
world—in this wonderful age;
for music and song and the human voice that can
reach me through the air;
for the redeeming, renewing gospel that comes
winged through space.

Bless this day, O God, all whose talents and energies
are thus devoted to you, and to the out-reach of your
Kingdom. AMEN

OUR PRAYER TOGETHER

From olden times, O God, men and women, with needs
not unlike our own, have listened to your voice:
Moses, the young shepherd, tending his father-in-
law's flocks beside the burning bush;
Abraham, ready to sacrifice his young son on an
altar of stones—till he heard you speak;
Isaiah, in a moment of worship within the Temple,
when your call came, 'Whom shall I send . . .?'

Make us today, O God, as responsive, however your
word comes to us. AMEN

EAGLE OF THE MATTERHORN

There was general rejoicing! The carpenter Geiger's family would reach thirteen in the end, but it never seemed difficult to find a name for a little new-comer. Though the name given Herman was not to be the one by which he would be widely known.

Young Herman might have been thought to lack a great many things which came to others; money was hardly earned by his father, and a good deal of contriving was called for. But, from early childhood, he never lacked spirit.

At fourteen, he started as a mechanic. And, despite the meagreness of his earnings, he managed to save. With time, and experience, he had enough to buy a little plane—a Piper Cub.

Now, he leads a squadron of twenty-three pilots—handling, all told, fifteen planes and three helicopters. And none of their flying is simple. They fly in the mountains—in the immense, hazardous mountains of Switzerland.

Among skiers and climbers, occasionally there are accidents. Then Herman and his colleagues are smartly on the job—with a record of some three to four hundred rescues a year. Emergency calls often start coming in as early as four in the morning. Fine days bring no fewer than stormy; indeed, good conditions often lead new-comers to risks they would not take at other times.

Stockily built, with a purposeful face, Herman has logged up thousands of miles in the mountains. His depot looks to some of us who have visited it of special interest for that reason—Sion happens also to be a very historical part of Switzerland. To its past, is now added a splendid present. For from this chosen starting-place, Herman has sought out two thousand landing-places in

the mountains, above a height of ten thousand feet. He
has learned to land his craft on high-altitude glaciers,
without coming to grief. And for this feat, he has earned
the nickname of which he is secretly proud: 'Eagle of
the Matterhorn'.

Approaching a target from below, he will skim over a
lip, and with neat judgment, halt on a sloping shelf—at
the exact instant swinging his machine sideways, to pre-
vent it sliding backwards. Herman's heart does not fail
him, though there is always the possibility that the
noise of his engine may start an avalanche.

Currents that he can use, reside in those high alti-
tudes in sun and in storm; but it takes courage and
experience to get an injured passenger down safely.

After thirty years of this service, a considerable
number of those who have come to the mountains owe
him their lives. Herman is modest about his record,
though he prizes in his secret heart a decoration from
Pope John. He is not a man of easy words; at most, he
can only be got to say smilingly, '*Ma fois*—it's my life!'

MY PRAYER
I give thanks, O God, at every thought of those who
hazard their lives for others—
    men of the mountains;
    fire-fighters, and ambulance men;
    train-drivers, and sea-captains.
I bless you for the selfless service—
    of doctors and nurses;
    scientists and researchers;
    parents and foster-parents.
Guard well this day, and this night, I pray—
    those whose occupations are dangerous;
    those high on new sky-scrapers;
    underground, in mines and tunnels;
    in factories and forges where molten metals flow.
Guard, too, all homes where little ones or old folk are—
    against scalds from spilled containers;

against electrocution;

against drowning in unsafe waterways.

So may the beauties of this wonderful world be shared without hurt; so may we go forth in eagerness and in your keeping, return each night in peace. To your glory. A M E N

OUR PRAYER TOGETHER

Gracious God, as the night draws about us, and the noises of the busy day are hushed, we would not forget those who still must work—

parents of sick children;

pilots in the air;

train-drivers boring a hole of light through the darkness.

Be especially kind to all who have the safety of others in their hands—

all who are responsible for young lives;

all who drive cars, and buses;

all who keep phones open in times of emergency.

We are thankful that we know more unselfish people than selfish; more happy home-keepers than those named in the court news; more loyal friends than disloyal; more happy people than miserable. Enable us to see things in perspective, and, as we can, to translate Christianity into daily living. With the shining truthfulness of your Kingdom let us live—showing forth the spirit of Christ, our Lord. A M E N

OUT-SPEEDING ANY DONKEY

Under the blue sky in St Peter Port, Guernsey, tiny waves lapped the bow of a fine craft. I found it hard to appreciate the *Flying Christine*'s battles with the elements. But speed, I knew, was in her make-up, as in the nature of Reg Blanchford himself. The moment the placid sea before me was whipped to fury, both would be tugging at their moorings to be off.

At fifteen, Reg's idea of speed, like that of many a lad, was a motor-bike. He badgered his father continually. But his youthful thrill when he opened up the throttle was short-lived. One dark, drizzly night, a collision with a taxi flung the young rider against the wall of a house, shattering both him and his machine.

The first man to pass the scene of the accident took in the situation. His instant reaction was to ring the ambulance—but in this case he knew it was of little use. There was only one ambulance on the island, serving a population of forty thousand, and its driver combined his duties with running a garage, and driving the fire-engine. So the passer-by got Reg into his own car. It wasn't ideal for one so hurt; and the first comment of the doctor, on their arrival at hospital, was 'This man is theoretically dead already'.

Reg was eight days unconscious, and an X-ray report showed: 'Frontal fracture of the skull, fracture of the lower jaw, three fractured ribs, fractures of the radius and ulna in the right wrist, fractured pelvis, two compound comminuted and complicated fractures of the right thigh-bone, crushed knee-cap, compound fracture of the right tibia, and a single fracture of the right fibula.'

When at last the youthful patient came round, he began to ask questions. Had the means of getting him to hospital worsened his loss of blood and his shock?

He got his answer—and gradually, during the next four years he spent under hospital care, a great idea was born. The island of Guernsey, he decided, should have the finest ambulance possible.

Reg's first need was to study as a recruit of the St John Ambulance Brigade. When able, Private Blanchford shakily made his way from door to door, begging subscriptions. He got 'ticked off' for exceeding his duties; but it made no difference.

The antiquated service still existed—but the new ambulance Reg secured had speed. And by the end of 1936, two thousand islanders were donating a shilling each a year; and, after three years, the parliament agreed to add £200 annually. It wasn't a lot, but 'the best ambulance service in the world' was on its way.

War brought the Nazi occupation of Guernsey. Petrol ran out—Reg resorted to charcoal as fuel. When this became scarce, he brought two horses and a specially prepared vehicle into service. When liberation came, no single call in those five years had gone unanswered. A blood bank was built up, and a radio-controlled ambulance and air-ambulance added.

Then came the smart sea-ambulance—the *Flying Christine*—which lay before my eyes that morning as I listened to its story. In a very short time she proved her worth. While Reg was on his way to church one morning in August 1950, the car radio came suddenly to life, and—instead of a family hour at worship with his wife and boys—he was away in a trice to bring off a cliff rescue.

Reg Blanchford holds today the George Medal, the M.B.E., the Queen's Commendation; the Life Saving Medal in gold of the Order of St John. But he finds most satisfaction in the truth inscribed on his Bronze Medallion of the Carnegie Hero Fund: '*He serves God best who most nobly serves humanity.*'

MY PRAYER

O Lord of life, I give thanks that you are always seeking out Good Samaritans to help you.

I give thanks that the spirit of that man upon the road down from Jerusalem to Jericho still lives.

I give thanks, too, that in this age, more effective means of help are available than a donkey, a flask of wine, and two pence.

Quicken in me, I pray, the living spirit of concern, where fellow-travellers in this life fall by the wayside.

Enlarge my practical knowledge, that, when the chance to help comes, I may not fail in readiness.

In this age of haste, with its small concern often for the needs of the individual, keep me sensitive;

Make me ready in whatsoever way is possible, separately, and along with others, to perpetuate the living spirit of the Good Samaritan.

And may the spirit and strength of Christ be my continual support, now and always. AMEN

OUR PRAYER TOGETHER

O Lord, we would examine our daily concern for others in the light of the faith we profess—

> words come at times so readily;
>
> actions so tardily;
>
> ancient, loved stories of the Gospels remain remote;
>
> the cost of meeting human need fails to excite us.

You have commanded us to love our neighbour as ourselves—

> though it may happen to be inconvenient;
>
> though the needy man turns out to be a stranger;
>
> though he has no family claim on us;
>
> though he turns out to be of another faith, another nationality.

Let us look quietly, honestly, at this story of the Good Samaritan—long enough to know where we come into the picture. AMEN

THE GREEN DREAM

The torturing heat and glare of the desert was hard to bear. Soil erosion spelt dust in the eyes, and hunger in the stomach. This deadly state of affairs followed on after the napalm bombs released by the French on the ancient forests strung round the neck of the Atlas Mountains.

Now the people were desperate. M. Jean Carbonare of the Christian Committee for Service in Algeria (backed by the World Council of Churches) for one, saw that something had to be done, and speedily. So, already a trained technician in several fields, he squared up to the challenge—though he had never before actually had anything to do with trees. The more he pondered on the dilemma of the people, the more sure he became that trees were the answer—eucalyptus trees, cedars, olives, pines, peaches, apples. Certain experts laughed at him—it would take far too long, they said. What would the poor people do in the meantime?

But M. Jean Carbonare had not jumped that question, any more than they had. Christian Aid, in England, would be as quick to see the point, and to promise practical aid. The first thing was to share the dream with the people's leaders on the spot; so the Government found itself soon, to its surprise, involved in a *Christian-Muslim dialogue*.

A small bunch of unemployed were sent out to what remained of the forests, so ancient that the Romans had hunted there the hyena, the wild boar, panther and jackal. All that green glory was now ruined; but here and there, with tireless eyes and ready fingers, the men managed to find fir-cones and other seeds. Another group of workers set about gathering up what soil they could, to make seed-beds.

After two years of unceasing work, they had twenty large seedling nurseries planted; and the 'green dream' was beginning to take recognizable shape. It was hot work, and unusual, for those taking part: tedious work in a temperature of 100° F.—hard work. Some sat hour after hour in the sketchiest of clothing—some in thick woollen army coats that had been sent them— parting seeds from husks, preparing tiny plastic soil-beds. Others moved from place to place, laboriously watering the tiny trees under the blistering sun. The women accepted a share in the project too, splitting long slithers from bamboo to make shields for the seedlings. Out on the rough, hot hills other workers fashioned terraces and prepared holes—one by one, thousands and thousands of them—each of a size to receive a seedling in a plastic pocket of soil.

Their immediate reward—on a rota of ten days at a time—was a slip of paper, offering food enough for six people for six weeks. As could be arranged, a C.C.S.A. lorry then visited village after village, and, for each hard-earned slip, left ninety kilos of semolina, a gallon of cooking oil, and six kilos of powdered milk.

Amidst proud chatter shared with his dependent family, and friends, sitting round the earthenware cook-ing-pot, a father here and another there might tell of his share in the green dream. Now he could, for the first time, feel certain that they could live. And one day, as certainly, his children's children would share the bene-fits of seventy million green trees in a land made new!

MY PRAYER

I can understand, O Lord of creation, a little of your joy—

> when you made the world;
> when you saw order come out of chaos;
> when light overcame darkness;
>> and life, death.

I rejoice for your breath given to men and women—
    for gifts of love and care;
    for daily work and developing skills;
    for guardianship of the earth and
        all your lesser creatures.
I grieve with you, that here and there this trust has been
dishonoured:
    where fertile soil has fallen to erosion;
    where laughing green acres have become
        deserts under the sun.
Quicken in men and women everywhere today a new
sense
    of stewardship; a new readiness to use
    their powers, and improved machinery,
    in the adventure of renewal.
So let the valleys and little hills sing and rejoice once
more; the barren places return to the peacefulness they
knew of old; the hunger of men and women and their
families be met—your will be done, and life be good!
Bless all who give their energies to hasten this day.

                                           A M E N

OUR PRAYER TOGETHER
O God, you have given so much to match the needs of
men and women—but not enough to match rapacious
greed;
    to match ignorance;
    to match want of leadership.
As news of conditions in many parts of the world
reaches us, let us not blame others for behaviour that
    matches our own;
    as stewards of the earth;
    as servants of your Kingdom.
We rejoice in technological advance—a gift from you
    that makes available new knowledge;
    that provides new mechanical tools;
    that makes possible the sharing of ill,
        and good, everywhere.

But most of all, our Father, we need a growth in your
spirit of

    generosity, if a better world is to be;
    grant us this greatest gift, we pray—
    in the name of Christ, our Master. A M E N

SPIRIT OF THE CARPENTER

It was the season of merciless heat and humidity. I stood at a busy corner, with the roar of traffic in my ears. The question was whether to take a rickshaw or a taxi?

When young Francis Yip first came to the site of the Church of the Holy Carpenter, there was no choice—and no church.

Throngs of refugees were pressing into Hong Kong —and he was one of them. Some were younger, some older—artisans, scholars, peasants, government-officials without offices, farmers without land, merchants without merchandise. And where were they all to find room —there was so little space in which to sleep and eat and live? The only hope of making more was to carve the tops off some of the stubborn, yellow hills, down to the level of the adjoining land, and dump the soil over into the sea.

Of the million-and-a-half men, women and children who had come crowding over the border, some set up flimsy shacks of scrap pieces of bamboo, slats of wood and oiled paper, rusty corrugated iron—cheek-by-jowl on precipitous hillsides still standing. Six- and seven-storey tenement blocks were planned—with thousands in each, five to each room. With water-taps at set points, and sanitation, these people would be immeasurably better off than the poor shanty-dwellers, subject to disease, typhoon floods, or fire. Thousands more found space on fishing-boats, and leaky old junks in the harbour.

The authorities, and the Church leaders were all very worried—Bishop Hall with the rest. In 1954, he got a stony hillside from the Government; and by honest sweat, fourteen unemployed youths levelled it in four and a half months. Tools were scarce, and they carried away the soil in coolie baskets. One of the youths was

Francis Yip. And on that precious piece of land, resulting from their levelling in Kowloon, I found him—a lithe, energetic, smiling minister in his early thirties, trained and ordained. It was a Monday—but he didn't know the meaning of 'Mondayish'. How could he? His church is the Church of the Holy Carpenter! A wonderful name—and a wonderful centre of life in its fullest sense.

On Sunday, he leads his people in worship—but for the whole seven days of the week, there is no line drawn between things sacred and secular. The life of the Holy Carpenter, our Lord—like the garment he wore—was a whole, woven without a seam. Beyond the altar is a finely carved figure of the Holy Carpenter of Nazareth, with hammer and chisel—the altar itself, fittingly, a carpenter's bench.

The seating, rearranged during the week-days, gives welcome to men from the docks, women from nearby homes and work-rooms, little children, youths and girls, for the matching of their daily needs. Yearly, some six hundred thousand meals are prepared and served there for a few cents each. Nearby stands a tall hostel—with two-tier bunks—for young workers; and work-shops and class-rooms, raised to match developing powers and energies, offer training in language, in dress-making, carpentry, spot-welding, spray-painting, and motor assembly, among a wide range of skills. And there are clinics and clubs, carving classes, social activities, and discussion-groups for others. The glorious, on-going truth about it is that life is all of a piece—worship and work—at the Church of the Holy Carpenter:

> Now is the holy not afar
>> In temples lighted by a star;
> Now that the King has gone this way,
>> Great are the things of every day!

MY PRAYER

O God, I am amazed and challenged by the ministry of

your Church in all the world!

I marvel at the widespread proof that you have made us for yourself,

and that our whole beings are restless, till we find our rest in your sustaining love.

You have laid your hands upon the whole of our natures—the whole of the time.

Forgive me that ever I have been unmindful of this great reality—

unaware that in you I live and move and have my being.

As your child in the world, quicken my imagination, that I may see how life here looks to others;

In my service to them, for your sake, let not my left hand know what my right hand does.

Teach me how to serve generously, and truly—without thought of either notice or praise. AMEN

OUR PRAYER TOGETHER

O Lord of life, turn our thoughts toward others today, and our hands to practical service;

let us add something worthwhile to this world—from the inspiration of our young Lord at the carpenter's bench;

> from his glorious rejection of the label 'sacred' and 'secular';
>
> from his teaching of the Family of God—and the prayer we still lisp, 'Our Father . . .';
>
> from his readiness to handle the servant's bowl, and wash others' feet.

We need and value these moments of solitude, when we can think about these things.

We find in the humble ministry of so many about us, true modern interpreters of Christ's spirit.

And we bless you for all these. Of your mercy, grant that we may be numbered among them in service today.

AMEN

JOYFUL JOHANNA

I can't remember a more exciting ride home than that night through the narrow, historic ways of old Jerusalem. Fresh-faced Johanna Larsen was at the wheel of the Volkswagen. We had just shared a meal together—but much more exciting, her good news! As many another might exclaim on returning home, 'I've just bought a hat!', her first eager words were, '*I've just bought the side of a mountain!*'

I questioned her about it. Star Mountain had been there so long, it seemed strange that it could be sold, or bought. Always, I learned, there had been lepers in Jerusalem, since our Lord's day. For a long time—despite his example of compassion, familiar to us all through the Gospels—very little was done for them. They spent their days in misery, keeping a legal distance; at night, they went into their hovels within the city walls, 'the huts of the unfortunate ones'.

About a hundred years ago—1867—a German lady on a visit to the city, was moved with compassion, and with others collected enough to build the lepers a home. The Moravian Church sent a German couple to be warden and housemother. Twenty years later, it had become too crowded to meet the need; and the compassionate Moravians built a bigger one. There, as many as sixty lepers were cared for at once.

But the home experienced good times and bad; and a blow more serious than any fell upon it in 1948, when it came under the control of the Jewish authorities at the Partition. In 1951, the sisters, and the lepers who chanced to be Arabs, left. The Church sisters could have gone back to Germany—but they elected to look after their unhappy dependants, who now took refuge in the Government leper-house in Siloam. The situation was such that those compassionate women found themselves wondering whether they should not give up.

The uneasy interval came to a close with that tremendous event that lit up Sister Johanna's face as she told me her news! No wonder she drove a little recklessly that night! On 12 June 1959, the foundation-stone of the new home was laid—bearing an unforgettable inscription in Arabic: *'Come unto me, all ye that labour and are heavy laden, and I will give you rest.'* Only one could utter those words, and, exactly a year later, a welcome in his name awaited all-comers on Star Mountain, near Ramallah. Neat quarters had been provided—for men on one side of the building, and for women on the other. Separate houses were available for married couples, with yet another solid stone building for the sisters and their guests.

And on this spot today—the leper home on Star Mountain, one of the most beautiful spots in Jordan— high in the Judean hills, this wonderful ministry continues. Each of the patients, young and old—the youngest but a boy—is lovingly tended by Sister Johanna and her helpers.

Tools have been provided so that the men who are able can share in the stone-gathering, the tilling, the planting of hundreds of little trees. Water is scarce, and would be even more so but for the mission donkey that carries it up on his back—four petrol-tins at a time— for the newly planted trees. Garden plants and tomatoes must depend on the dew to meet their needs.

Here—under the blue vault of heaven that Christ knew—in his troubled land today, his words, inscribed on a foundation-stone, have living significance: *'Come unto me, all ye that labour and are heavy laden, and I will give you rest.'*

MY PRAYER
Gracious God, I hush my heart in wonder at all I know of you—through Jesus Christ—

when men and women cared little for sufferers;
when lepers were especially feared, and chased
away;
when the poor and wretched were left alone under
the stars;
when almost nothing effective was known in the
way of a cure.

I give thanks for all new knowledge of drugs and treatments for the suffering of my fellow men and women.

I give thanks for all tender hearts and skilled hands set to interpret compassion today.

I give thanks for the prayers and the money-gifts of all who share in this ministry.

You have given me so much—show me how best I can express my thanks for health and wholeness.

In the spirit of Christ. AMEN

OUR PRAYER TOGETHER

O God, our Father, we raise our humble prayer for all who suffer today—
bodily pain, temporary or chronic;
fear of tomorrow and a worsening of things;
loneliness or ostracism.

O God, we seek your help, too, for all who lack wholeness of mind
and spirit, as well as health of body;
all who lack knowledge of Christ's compassion.

When the clamour of this busy day dies, and darkness gathers us in to
restful sleep,
draw especially near, we pray, to the very sick, to
the sleepless, to the dying.

Match the needs of all for whom we pray, with your sustaining grace
and renewal, O God,
here, or in the life just beyond our human sight.

AMEN

FRIEND OF ALL THE WORLD

I was as widely awake as any beneath those cloud-flecked blue Swiss skies—though I had climbed to a 'dream'. The Children's Village had taken shape, I knew, in the heart of a young Swiss doctor, Dr Walter Corti, during a time when he was ill in hospital. He had begun his career as a specialist in brain research; then it was discovered that he had tuberculosis. A great part of Europe, just then, lay ravaged by war, and the world, mad with mixed national purposes and powers, seemed to him, as he thought of it in his depression, hardly a world worth living in. Throngs of homeless, frightened people—many of them children—were on the roads. Dr Corti couldn't get them out of his thoughts. He wrote to the newspapers, urging that, whatever could be done for the adults, the children should be helped first.

In their peaceful little mountainous country, he reminded his readers, children in the past had found help in the compassionate heart of Pestalozzi—his monument, showing him bending low to listen to a child, stood on a little patch of grass, in Zurich. 'Can we not show his spirit, today?' asked Corti. For by this time, he was pulling out of his depression, his dream taking shape.

Now it stands realized—a children's village for little ones from all over Europe—named after that good man Pestalozzi. Corti had begun collecting for it whilst still in his hospital bed. He felt there was need for haste. The nurses who tended him smiled at the tobacco-tin with a hole in its top—but they spared a few coins. One day he handed round a notebook into which he had written words that in time would be part of the UNESCO charter: 'Since wars begin in the minds of men, it is in the minds of men that the defences of peace must be constructed.' A beginning might well be made with the children.

And much more he did—when he got out of hospital. A piece of land was found with fresh mountain air and sun, among friendly neighbours. The small village of Trogen, in the canton of Appenzell, sixty-odd miles east of Zurich, promised to be ideal. And on that green hillside the children's village was raised.

The first-comers soon began to arrive—children from Austria, Poland, France; then others from Greece, Finland, Switzerland and Britain. The people of Trogen, they found, spoke German—so they learned to speak it, too. In no time they were eagerly immersed in lessons and games, in music and handcrafts of their many countries. And when Winter brought its mantle of snow, the glorious experience of skiing was waiting to be shared. Winter sports found many enthusiasts, in what was then 'the only international children's village in existence'.

And still—in every part of their life—*family* interests come first there, each national group of sixteen or so in its own charming house, with experienced houseparents. Wherever possible, the young folk return to their countries of origin for summer holidays, to help them grow up, not 'vague internationalists', but useful citizens of their own nation, with an international outlook. From the beginning, they are encouraged to keep birthdays and Christmas and other festivals, and to share in worship. '*You must always be brothers and sisters*', the opening words of one of their favourite songs ring out, for those of the great world who will listen.

And we are left wondering when all the world will learn to sing it.

MY PRAYER
O God, it is wonderful to realize that though you set galaxies in space, hold the pulsing tides, and the comings and goings of the seasons, you care more for human lives—

that you have made us each in your own image;
and set within each of us capacity for worship, joy,
and wonder;
for the fashioning of dreams;
for free thought;
for service.
Grant to me a proper sense of values—
deliver me this day from the servitude of things;
enable me to discover the lasting joy of giving;
save me from an ambitious life-plan, wanting in
service;
deliver me this day from casualness and unconcern.
So may the spirit of Christ possess me wholly, his dreams
be my dreams, his joy be my joy.

Let no unexpected demand of the passing hours find
me wanting in his compassion, and lasting love. AMEN

OUR PRAYER TOGETHER
Gracious Lord, it is both comfort and challenge that
none of our private thoughts just now come as a surprise
to you—
so we want to bare our hearts in sweet honesty;
to ask your forgiveness for our ignorance, where
knowledge is readily available;
to claim your promise of power to keep our minds
adventurous;
to live as part of your great world-family.
Save from despair, O God, those who must travel a hard
way;
teach us how best to translate our concern into
action;
deliver us from hasty judgments;
let us persevere to replace war with peace, evil of
all kinds with goodness, drabness with beauty.
So may this torn world that so many children inherit,
become a place of righteousness and joy. In the name
of Christ our Lord. AMEN

A VISION SHARED WITH MILLIONS

I drew aside the curtains at the window of my seventeenth-floor room. Chicago's special shapes pressed in upon me—chief to claim attention, the tallest spire in the world. Five hundred and sixty-eight feet of it rose up from a Methodist church. Chicago Temple, I was to discover, stands rock-based in the heart of the city's 'down-town loop'—high over all, its lighted cross against the sky; the call of its chimes above the struggle and din; its 'Sky Sanctuary', a little chapel four hundred feet above human wisdom. Beneath the chapel is the minister's four-roomed 'Sky Parsonage'. A considerable part of the whole building is set aside for offices.

Next morning, when my feet took me through its open doors, I found its sanctuary crowded. It affords seating for twelve hundred; and half that congregation was in the eighteen to forty age-group, as the preacher and pastor, Dr Charles Goff, reminded me.

Many week-day activities, as well as Sunday morning and evening worship, spell out warm fellowship in that so often lonely, heartless city. Somebody, I could see, had taken time, human skill, and money, to make the whole building beautiful—conducive to worship, in support of the spoken word, music of choir and organ.

Later, Dr Goff drew my attention to the particular gift of one man—artist Warner Sallman—a large framed copy of his *Head of Christ*. I knew it from a tiny print on my study wall at home—one of sixty million copies today, the world round. It shows Christ young—as indeed he was—timeless, strong. Sallman, Dr Goff took pleasure in telling me, made his picture available for the narthex, through which thousands pass daily to their offices—and with good reason.

Many years earlier, the Doctor had led a series of

lunch-hour studies in the Chicago Y.M.C.A. Among the young men attending, listening silently, was Warner Sallman. One day, Dr Goff caused him to think of Christ in a new way. It started the young man sketching, as the discussion went on. That night his sketch seemed to come alive, and be rounded out, as in a dream. To capture it on paper, he got out of bed. Next day he completed it. It was published later as the front cover of a church magazine.

When Dr Goff started his search for a picture suitable for the narthex, a preacher-artist told him of Sallman's *Head of Christ*, and he wrote to the artist for an interview. 'When I went to his studio', said Dr Goff, 'I was completely surprised to see my young acquaintance of years gone by. I said to him, "You did not paint that picture, did you?" He replied, "No, I have been waiting all these years to tell you that you gave me that picture." When I asked him how that could possibly be, he said, *"But you gave Christ to me."* '

And, in his turn, Warner Sallman—with his dedicated skills—brings to men and women in countless churches, class-rooms and homes today the world around, his awareness of the living Christ.

MY PRAYER

Eternal God, I marvel at the things you do in this world, through dedicated men and women.

Already, you have made with exceeding beauty the earth in which you have set us;

You have set its gaseous and rocky framework beyond my imagination;

You have wrought mightily, through darkness and light, the sun and the moon and the miracle mass of stars;

The mountains, the seas, the trees, and every least thing of grass and garden, bless you!

But lovelier, and more lasting than the laws of nature, you have quickened the inmost longings of my heart.

In your holy presence words fail me again and again, and I keep wondering silence before you.

I give praise, above all I know of your nature, for your good on-going purposes in this world, through Jesus Christ.

I rejoice that clothed in senses five, he shared our human life, dealt with people as he found them, amid real situations.

I take courage to approach you, because of what he showed us of you, of your love, and care, and hope, and greatness.

I give thanks for the scribes who with eagerness wrote down these things in the Gospels.

I give thanks continually for all writers since, who have made the Gospels better understood—all translators, illustrators, teachers, all preachers, lecturers.

I give thanks for all artists, who, like Sallman, dedicate themselves to your service.

Let my life be as beautiful within, my gaze as steady, my inmost values as sure as those of the Christ he has shown me. AMEN

OUR PRAYER TOGETHER
O God, where there is ugliness, ignorance and distrust, let men come by a clearer vision of you, in Jesus Christ—

Let love reach out in genuine understanding; let courage match the challenge; let hope overmaster despair.

Where people are tired, frustrated, sad, give them a new sense of your companionship, in Christ.

Where the young seek leaders, let them not pass you by—since you have designed us for joyous wholeness of being.

We cannot realize our secret dreams without you—so seek us out, love us, and keep us, that we may truly live. AMEN

NIGHT LIFE IN NAPLES

Little Mario was at the beck and call of all in the barber's shop. 'Mario do this, Mario do that, Mario go and fetch a black coffee, a white coffee, a glass of anise!' And, but eight years of age, he would dash into the streets.

There was no hint then that his life's greatest adventures would be in those same streets, part of the nightmare of Naples' slums. There, he would come to know well the *scugnizzi*, the virtually parentless— roaming by night, robbing under cover of darkness, sleeping where they chose on pieces of waste newspaper, among the rats and vermin. Mario's start was above that of most—in a family of five, with five more having died in infancy. His father had followed the trade of a silver-gilder; a brother was a jeweller; and various sisters and aunts helped with the burnishing of pieces, traditionally women's work. But do what they could— separately and together—they lived on the edge of poverty.

Into the barber's shop where little Mario picked up a few coins, came one day a priest, Don Nobilione. In a short while, he was to become the lad's hero. And Mario—thirteen years old—was seized by the ambition to be a priest himself. His hero paid for his early education.

By 1946—still small of stature, pale, but trained in part—the young priest emerged, Don Mario Borrelli. He knew himself dedicated to save some of the homeless urchins from the alleyways, engulfed in misery, disease, corruption and active crime.

At first, there was the great problem of winning confidence. Police-scared, priest-scared, it could never be easy, he knew. And some were vicious, and carried razors. Their would-be friend would have to share their precarious existence by night, but before that, persuade his Church superiors that this was a thing not too dangerous to do. His only hope of helping the urchins was to become an urchin—following on into the city after he had done his priestly duties by day—in ragged pants, cap and greasy coat, his shabby boots tied with string. But even that was not enough. He had to stop shaving, to learn their slang, and to loosen his controlled temper, in order to allay suspicion. But before any of these things could happen, he had to find a gang that would accept him. His smallness of stature helped—but he had to earn his acceptance by collecting scrap-papers for bedcoverings; and orange-skins, boot-soles and combustible garbage to burn in a rusty old can that could provide a little warmth at night. Their main source of finance—a few *lire* at a time to add to what they stole—came from collecting cigarette-butts off the street. Some they allowed themselves to smoke to stave off hunger, the rest they sold. It meant night-work always because then the wheeled traffic of the city was less, though with the quickest eyes it took at least two thousand stoops to pick up enough dirty butts for a kilo of tobacco. Water-front bars, night-clubs, gambling dens, bus-stops, were best, and women's fag-ends more generous than men's—they didn't smoke them down so far.

Mario managed to do with three hours' disturbed sleep —thanks to lice, cold, hunger, and boys' coughs—and his daily work found him all but exhausted. All the time it was essential that he keep his dual life a deadly secret.

At last, the day came when he felt that he was well enough established to be able to declare himself, and invite some with whom he had made real friends to an old, altarless church that was due for renovation—to what came to be known as the House of Urchins, *Casa dello Scugnizzo.*

And, greatly expanded, this incredible life-saving service continues to this hour—a stab of light in the nightmare of Naples!

MY PRAYER

I am humbled to hear of men and women who believe that nothing is too hard for you—

> young and old, who give themselves to the utmost;
> who minister in ways that nobody knows about;
> who minister in ways that everybody knows about.

I bless you for your living Church in the world—

> deliver me from forms of self-praise when I help a little;
> enable me to step aside from accepted ideas, if I can serve the better;
> sustain my effort when the newness and novelty of any venture has died.

So may I spend myself in your service, seeking no reward but your glory. In the spirit of Christ who did this so superbly, my Lord. AMEN

OUR PRAYER TOGETHER

Source of every good and splendid thing, O God, we worship you with our whole selves. Set us where you will, let us serve as we can.

We would not think of prayer as an easy way of service—asking, 'Do what we want.' Rather would we ask, 'Do with us what you want.'

O God, we're ashamed that so often our self-giving is so slender, our love so small, even our motives so mixed.

O Father, hold close to your heart each prodigal in the 'far country'—with passions strong, and will too weak to keep him straight;

Grant the day may come when he turns his face toward home—toward confession of a foolish choice;

Forgive him, and let us, on his return, forgive him as freely, and bring forth the best robe of a son, a ring, and shoes. And let us together make merry and rejoice with you. AMEN

FISHING IN THE DESERT

A skinny water-seller trundled his doubtful supply through the streets of Aden. There had not been rain for many months. That most-used port of Arabia, under the ancient, merciless, shimmering heat, was the more cruel for that. Standing at the end of a rocky peninsula, it kept company with arid rocks, and the centre of an extinct volcano.

Out beyond came an illusion that belongs to the desert—a generous, refreshing, green pool, palm-fringed it looked. But of course it was a mirage. And all the tales I had read of travellers lured on, and eventually lost in the desert when each shimmering pool of this kind disappeared, struck me afresh.

I came upon the same phenomenon in the merciless desert heart of Australia—a thousand miles from the sea. And I heard grim stories of men lost there, seeking a pool where no pool existed at all.

The originator of the old saying, 'Seeing is believing', had obviously no experience of a desert; the criss-crossing of streaks of light, which, from the beginning, have lured men to exhaustion and death, told another tale. Water in the desert was hard to find—the mirage's deception general.

So when Inter-Church Aid headed a bulletin covering a special piece of refugee work 'Fishing in the Desert', I was sceptical. There was no fishing without water; this could only be a mirage story, the writer suffering from 'a touch of the sun'. But I read on: 'In one of the hottest, driest, and most savage deserts in the world, Church workers are helping build up a fishing co-operative which aims at producing a hundred thousand rainbow trout a year. These', I read, my eyebrows rising, 'will add badly needed protein to the diet of a

depressed community . . . It is a lunar landscape—
fantastic, barren and menacing. There is no rain. Only
here and there, spaced out many miles apart, are a few
small, green oases where the presence of fresh water
has enabled trees to grow and some sparse crops of
maize, beans and alfalfa.'

Fishing in the desert? In this kind of desert—a mirage,
surely? But no! In the last few years, some thousands
of inhabitants have been added to Calama, the largest
settlement in this Chilean wasteland, to work in the
near-by copper mine. Most have had to content themselves with shacks made of scrap—cardboard, old sacks,
and sheets of rusty tin. A fantastic setting!

Justo Maccario, an Argentinian agronomist and veter-
inarian who had arrived in this strange settlement, was
not one to forget that the new inhabitants were men
and women with basic needs like his own. But when
he met, soon after his arrival, two men walking across
the desert towards him carrying fishing-rods and four-
teen-pound rainbow trout, he could only think himself
suffering 'a touch of the sun', and what he saw 'a
mirage'. But no!

On sober investigation, the stream which he had
planned to use for irrigation, to produce food for the
needy people, proved to be so saline that it was useless.
Then Maccario learned how an American executive at
the mine, during his spell of service, had stocked the
stream with trout to relieve the tedium of his leisure-
time with a little fun. He had since returned to head-
quarters in his homeland—but fish still multiplied in
the saline stream! The moment Maccario—pinching
himself—met those two rod-carrying men in the desert,
a great new plan formed in his mind. The saline stream
proved exactly the water for trout! And, fantastic as his
first report sounded, Inter-Church Aid, without loss of
time, set about plans to increase the six ponds already
providing fish to a hundred by the end of the year!
And a seeming mirage now gives way to a miracle!

MY PRAYER

O God, never morning wears to evening, but some surprise visits us men and women, some good is done.

I thank you for the amazing variety of the earth's surface—for the green fields, hills, and deserts.

I rejoice in the gentle dews, and rains which bless our sowing in farms and gardens.

I rejoice in the beauty and variety of grass and trees and flowers.

Let me not forget those in arid places, where food enough for existence is a struggle.

Grant wisdom and strength to all who toil far from home, that others may be served.

Bless the servants of great societies like Inter-Church Aid, that exist solely to help the needy, in the name of Christ, our Lord. AMEN

OUR PRAYER TOGETHER

O God, let the sacredness of human life be ever real to us—especially in this impersonal age;

in this hungry world;

in the expression of our faith in you.

O God, you have fashioned us to live together as members of your human family;

with varied gifts and talents;

with differing experiences;

in every part of the earth.

Together, we would raise our prayer—'Give us this day our daily bread';

and we would offer our energies;

and our gathered experience;

to enable you to answer that prayer. AMEN

A DREAMING YOUTH

Squinting into blunt rain, the small newspaper-boy sought what shelter he could in an open doorway. Jimmy Butterworth was eldest of five—his mother a widow. He went to work at twelve—leaving home at five in the morning for a foul bleach works four miles away, returning at seven. Since his wage was three shillings and ninepence a week (with a penny deducted for hot water to make tea), he sold newspapers on the way home, to augment the family income. Poverty and loneliness, grim twins, stalked the bleak Lancashire moors, and many a crowded back street on their rims. *Somewhere for a boy to go—someone to be with*—made up, as he remembers now, a basic need, persisting all through his efforts to organize village football; to raise his voice in chapel as a young preacher; and his spell in France with mud-weary Lancashire Fusilier Bantams in World War I.

One bright memory remained—of the time when Queen Mary made an appearance in the near-by town of Accrington. Pavement crowds, pushing away from Jimmy's smelly bleach garments, afforded him in doing so, a better view than many had that day. 'One day', said he to himself, 'that lovely lady will open my Clubland!' And years later, Her Majesty did so!

The young dreamer became a Methodist theological student; and, in time, found himself sent to London to do what he could with a run-down 1813 chapel, with but a few stalwarts attending. Little did any one of them care that round about their dingy streets were hundreds of youngsters—thinking many of the same thoughts that Jimmy himself had struggled with a few years before. Not one of the stalwarts—even when won over to 'the

dream'—could have guessed that today, half a century
later, their young parson would still be there, 'where the
action is'. Disconsolate slum pigeons perched high on
grubby ledges looking into courtyards, broken chimney-
pots adding to the murk. In time, the old chapel was
brought to the ground—lest it fall down—and the
'dream' began to grow. One lad, Patrick, confessed to
Jimmy that he was planning more crimes in order to get
back to Reform School where friends and football could
be had. As things turned out, he got himself into prison
instead. But his plight proved to be one more experience riveting the youthful founder-head of Clubland to
his human task.

Some years later, I threaded my way through its
sordid surroundings one Sunday night. I found, to my
surprise, a beautiful building. The famous architect of
Guildford Cathedral, Sir Edward Maufe, R.A., had designed a fit setting for the practical service, and ideals of
Clubland. That night—worship led by two teenagers, a
boy and girl, in neat club gowns, the head preaching
briefly—has stayed in my mind ever since.

It had been arranged that juniors might join at ten,
seniors at fourteen—and at this date thousands have
passed through to highly qualified, responsible service
in many walks of life—in Medicine, Architecture, Law,
Education, Business, the Church, the Theatre, etc. From
time to time, they come back to renew associations and
to support new projects. Reaching out into the wide
world, Clubland is 'a home of friendship'. Within, dis-
cussions go on endlessly and there are such activities as
gym, handcrafts, drama, dancing, art, films; and out of
doors there are athletics, cycle-trips, sports, camps.

Suddenly, in 1941, heartless air-raids destroyed the
beloved buildings. Many of the young folk were already
evacuees, a number were old enough to be in the
forces. The skeleton group patched up parts not totally
demolished—setting up an altar under the sky. Sad
days!

But, in 1946, Queen Mary returned—to inaugurate a rebuilding scheme. It was to prove costly, and lengthy: twenty-five years were to pass before Clubland would again stand complete—hostels, clubs and chapel—under the London sky. And under the redoubtable leadership of Jimmy Butterworth, grown grey in fifty years of service to youth, Clubland today holds its splendid purpose, and its many friends—royal friends, friends distinguished in the Arts, and in Business, humble friends, generous, regular. And the spontaneous tribute of a Clublander to their beloved founder-head still speaks truth: '*You made us believe you could build anything with us, but nothing without us!*'

MY PRAYER

O Lord of life, just where I am, lead me to expend my energies in building up, rather than in breaking down.

I rejoice in your building skill—early, in the carpenter's shop in Nazareth—and, to this hour, in human lives.

Youth affords you still fine building stuff—so that warped natures can be made straight, and the weak be made strong.

I bless you for the 'dreams' of youth—for splendid creative gifts of trust and friendship.

In your Kingdom is no 'generation-gap'; no exclusiveness of sex, colour or clime.

You have shown this to me again and again—despite contradictory experiences, and frustrations.

Grant that my daily relationships with youth may be worthy of your lasting love and respect and hope for us all. AMEN

OUR PRAYER TOGETHER

Eternal Father, we would look up to you, that young people may look up to us.

In giving us the capacity to worship, you have set us far above the creatures of forest and field.

In fashioning us for lasting fellowship with yourself, you have made of our life here an enriching adventure.

Receive our thanks, and in every situation where we find ourselves today, undergird our insufficiency. In Christ's name. A M E N

A ONE-WHEELED MIRACLE

Life in the mountains for a little handful of Greek
families will never be the same again. It is still hard
enough to get a living in Elaphos. Ioannis Raptis and his
family are typical. They struggle to do what they can
with two-and-a-half acres of valley and stony mountain
slope. They own two goats, one cow and a donkey. Now
—thanks to the World Council of Churches—they have
a part-share in a wheelbarrow!

When it turned up, there was great excitement; no
one in the village had seen anything like it. The fathers
of the village took turns in handling it. With such un-
even, stony ground, it wasn't easy; but somehow they
managed to push it forward in wobbly fashion. The
children begged rides.

The CROP section of the World Council of Churches
hadn't of course, provided the new tool solely for excitement. It was for work; and always in Elaphos there
is plenty of that. One of Ioannis Raptis' two sons is
away in the great city—a welder in Athens; the other
helps on the little mountain farm. A daughter, married,
lives near-by. The work they share between sunrise and
darkness is decided by the passing seasons—in spring
begins the hoeing, sowing and hoping. The sky then is
blue, and the sun already quickening life. With the
passing of time, there are other routine jobs—the house
to repair after the rain-storms, garments to knit from
the limited stock of wool available, meals to keep going,
tools to mend, goats to tend lest they stray as they graze
on the mountainside.

Only Sunday is different. Then the people put on
their simple best, and go together to the church for worship. Their minister is too poor to be able to give all
his time to ministering—he has to work much of his

time in the fields. And at night, when most, tired out, have gone to their beds, he sits up, and by the light of an old oil-lamp, prepares for the following Sunday. But somehow he manages, and the people of Elaphos get what their hearts need from their worship.

Every now and again, a crazy bus climbs up the winding roads to the village, bringing a passenger or two, and goods to meet certain needs. But for the rest, the outside world seems to care little about them. That is not counting Demos—a fellow-Greek, a strong helper from the World Council of Churches. Demos believes that Christianity must express itself in practical ways, close to life. So he has been glad to introduce the precious wheelbarrow, to bring also tools and seeds. And, when the planting ends, to set himself to help wheel up building materials for Ioannis to put a much-needed new kitchen on to his house—handier, weather-proof, and so better for the health of his family. A great many common things in the village are now better—thanks to Demos.

It was only natural, perhaps, that one Sunday—after having heard the Scriptures read: '*Freely ye have received, freely give!*'—one, speaking for all, as they came out of Church, should ask of Demos: 'How can we help others?' And this miracle in the village started with a wheelbarrow!

MY PRAYER
O God, I thank you for good men from the beginning, eager to transmit your aid to their fellows in need—
    prophets who were not halted by unpopularity;
    preachers and scribes, who shared your words;
    handy-men and practical helpers, ready to bend to
      your tasks.
I thank you that these are still in the earth—
    spelling out relief, and simple progress;
    interpreting loving-care;
    stirring in grateful hearts an on-going response.

Bless today all who in any way give themselves to
their fellows,

to build up good and wholesome life;

to share mundane tasks for far-reaching ends;

to do your holy will in the world of men and things.
Out of your bounty, you have given us more than we
have desired, or deserved; give us one gift more—thankful hearts. Give to those of us starting out in life, clear-sighted purpose; to the middle-aged, patience with faults
and follies; and to the old, with the mellowing of the
years, generosity of spirit. So may we each serve you,
and praise you, in our lives day by day. In Christ's spirit.

AMEN

OUR PRAYER TOGETHER

We pray today, O God, for little people in large societies
—and for all, who, for your sake, seek them out, and
go to their aid.

We pray for ventures of loving care, of which the big
world hears little through its news-media—for fashioners of tools; planters of trees and seeds.

We pray for people in back-room jobs—laboratory
staff; domestic helpers in over-full hospitals; in old
people's homes; demonstrators in agricultural projects.

Grant to these, we pray, your strong creative gifts of
persistence. Bless especially, all who face a crisis without the support of loved ones; all who have no human
help to call on.

Teach us how to make a better thing of our own living
and loving—and let us not fail in the task close at hand
—carried away by the far need of which we hear. AMEN

COURAGE AND COMPASSION

When Geoffrey Leonard Cheshire—as his name appeared on the records—left Stowe School, little could he have guessed what life held in store for him. Nor was there any hint of it when he left Merton College, Oxford. All that was coming into focus was the grim fact that external powers were mounting for conflict in the safe world he knew.

Rejoicing in his youthful energies and enthusiasms, Cheshire was just twenty-one when war broke out. On the day it was declared, he dashed off eagerly into Oxford and bought a dozen rabbit snares. The idea was that his parents might catch themselves sufficient meat, if ever regular supplies should be cut off. It was hard to tell what the future held. Then, he came back and dug a couple of shelters—one near the house in a little pine wood that might afford some cover, one out in the middle of a field.

As soon as he was able, he joined the R.A.F. At first, this involved the signing of all manner of tedious papers, and as many journeys. Finally, in October, he got into flying school. He was in a typical youthful hurry, though as yet, there was no visible sign of the place and form of enemy action. His sole aim was to be 'a good pilot'.

After what seemed an interminable time, he began to get postings—one on the other side of the Atlantic, to wait for a Hudson in Montreal, and ferry it back to England. It wasn't ready on his arrival, and in typical high spirits—without permission or passport—he hitched a ride to New York, dream-city of his imagination.

But war was no game; and things took a grim turn. He was involved in operations for which he had trained

—night-flying, and hazardous decisions. An hour came when his own brother—two years younger—went missing. Fog had closed in over the whole country, creating anxiety in many hearts, and the loss of forty Bomber Command aircraft. Fortunately, young Christopher managed to get down. Later, on his twenty-third trip, he failed to return—and turned up later in a prison-camp. It *was* serious.

Geoffrey Leonard was posted here, there—promoted. War was now being waged with costly intensity. He was appointed to command the 617 Squadron—the famous Dambusters. One night late, at a celebration with friends, a girl unexpectedly leaned across the table where they sat, and asked: 'How much do you know about God?' Some of the company laughed; but not Cheshire. He knew it was a relevant question, and that a real person was involved. He had gone to church, as a boy, because he had been made to; he had done the accepted Divinity at school, and passed exams. But no one could count these very real. And this was a time for reality above all.

One ghastly experience that he would never forget was being chosen, among others, as official British observer of the atomic bomb dropped on Nagasaki, when so many Japanese perished.

Cheshire was loaded with medals for outstanding service—the V.C., D.S.O. (with two bars), and the D.F.C. In 1946 he retired from the Service, to discover many sitting around in like positions, complaining about life in general. This was a great test of character, but Cheshire's reaction was positive.

'Why not get up and act?' he asked himself, and others, through a widely read newspaper. Letters began to pour in—till, with help, he was able to set about the first Cheshire Foundation Home for the Incurably Sick. Since that time, many other such have been set up in Britain, in Europe, and in the Far East. Today—devout

Catholic, husband, father, friend—he continues this splendid service, matching courage with compassion.

MY PRAYER

O God, giver of health of body and mind, I cannot imagine myself without these gifts—
so I give you thanks for all who minister to the sick;
all who spend generously their time and substance;
all who seek to restore to the incurable a sense of dignity.

Let me not forget those reduced to walking-sticks, calipers, wheel-chairs and sick-beds;

Let me not forget those who morning after morning seem to have little to look forward to;

Let me not forget those who must go on suffering, in ways few of us can imagine, at times few of us know.

Support and encourage today, all builders of special homes—all raisers of funds, all administrators and staff.

These things I ask, because none other can give these essential gifts—in the name of the Great Physician, Christ. AMEN

OUR PRAYER TOGETHER

It surprises us, O God, to find how easy it is to be casual about the crippled, the sick, when we don't see them—

It surprises us how easy it is to leave provision for them to the specialists, and dash around on our own concerns;

It surprises us how easy it is to dismiss our carelessness with neat excuses that don't convince anyone—least of all, you—

For so many of us this is the 'age of the shrug'.

All too many of us—in Cheshire's words—'overlook the power of the little act'.

Deliver us, O God, from this selfishness—
Let Christ's spirit lay hold of us.

Show us, here and now how we can help—
Lest our interest evaporate in words and fruitless
   sentiment.
We seek these blessings in the name of Christ, our
Lord. A M E N

PAPA SANTI

It was Riccardo Santi's birthday, and he was going
home. As a pastor, he lived with his wife and family in
a tiny apartment above the first Methodist church in
Naples. That day, in an archway, he came upon two
little street-hawkers and, he said, God whispered in his
ear, 'Take these children home for me, and care for
them. And I will never forsake you!'

At once his wife wondered however they would manage. They already had an aged grandmother to care
for. True, the church people kept in mind their small
means. Some—like Angelo and Rosetta—came under
their kindly roof from the slums of the city; some from
villages devastated by an eruption of Vesuvius; some
from parts of Sicily destroyed by earthquake. Soon the
two children became a dozen.

In a short time, 'Papa Santi'—as the children came
to call him—had to look for more room. Ten years on,
they were again overcrowded, with more than eighty
children. After the head of the house had outlined their
position at a conference he was privileged to attend, the
American Methodist Board of Missions offered some
much-needed help. Moved to continuing interest, two
of their number later paid a visit to Naples. They were
riding in a taxi there, when they fell to speaking about
'Papa Santi's family' being so overcrowded. The kindly
taxi-driver replied that he knew a place that might help,
and could drive them to it. It proved to be a princely
villa in seven acres of grounds in Portici, stretching
away down towards the blue Bay of Naples. It had two
main buildings on that idyllic spot—a farm-house,
stables and coach-house—and belonged to the Prince of
Monaco. And they were able to arrange for its use by
the children.

But Santi's problems were not yet at an end. Though they had now space enough for beds, lessons and games, money was slow to come in. And a day came when Papa Santi had to go round thinking what they could spare—picking out a chair here and a chest there. But before carrying these bits of furniture off to the dealers, he called his staff and youthful family to prayers. He had not forgotten the promise made him at the outset—though he well knew he had himself to do all he could. In the prayer-time there came a loud knock. It proved to be a German helper back, who had left in a 'huff' because of something said in a sermon. Now he was knocking, full of apologies—and with a handsome gift of money in an envelope, enough to cover back-rent, with some left over for months to come.

The family of Casa Materna was a little Protestant island of life in a predominantly Catholic population of some established thousands. Understandably, it took time to get to know each other—much more to trust each other, help each other. But that good time came, despite a day when some were set on closing Casa Materna, till a high-court action defeated their objective. Next, war descended, and bombs fell, and the children had to be hurried into hiding. But that, too, passed.

And by now, nine thousand in all have found themselves part of 'Papa Santi's family', which faces life sturdily, led today by two of his honoured sons, each with a training their father never knew—but with the same tender care. *At Casa Materna Love takes no holidays*!

MY PRAYER
O Lord of life, who has wrought the world with exceeding beauty, I bless you for all tender things of grass and garden;

  for living creatures—pets, and birds of the air;

especially for little children, dependent and loving;
I bless you for all who have shown themselves worthy
of such trust—

    in the home, growing amid lessons, games and
        laughter;

    in foster-homes and institutions, and among neigh-
        bours;

    in health and sickness—in hospitals; and wherever
        needs are met, and love is returned.

Let me show reverence this day for the bodies, minds
and spirits of all with whom I have to do.

You have fashioned our hearts to care, our hands
to create, our spirits to journey on with courage and
joy.

You have given us games to play, and books to read,
and set pure laughter on our lips.

Let the lasting values of Christ—simplicity, honesty,
helpfulness, good faith—be part of my ministry this
day;

In the name of him who glorified childhood as a
member of a working man's family in Nazareth. A M E N

OUR PRAYER TOGETHER
Let no sense of our well-being, O God, blind us to the
need of many young things growing up today. Most of
us find it easier vaguely to love the whole world than
one individual child—

    this takes much time;

    this takes sustained interest;

    this takes much understanding.

Daily we are worried by newspaper pictures of little
ones with glazed eyes and pot-bellies—refugees from
war, natural disasters, famine—

    we cannot forget them;

    we have to feel in our pockets;

    we have to mention them in our prayers.

But we are busy people, and someone else soon comes

to crowd them out. We find it less costly to deal with things than with persons—question-posing children; reckless youth; lonely, time-consuming adults. But somehow—since we bear our Lord's Name—we know we must learn to express his living compassion. Teach us how to live his way. AMEN

NEW READERS, NEW WRITERS

With the ticking-by of each minute, our workaday world has a hundred new readers; but against a pitiful background of seven hundred million illiterates!

' "Operation-upgrade" sounded fine when first we heard about it in church,' Mrs Sliedrecht admitted, when I questioned her about the Indian families at the explosives factory. 'Exciting, even! But I wasn't in any way interested when I was asked to do something about it.' And I could understand—it sounded rather like 'Operation Babel', with Mrs Sliedrecht from Holland being challenged to teach Indian employees in an African explosives factory!

'The first chance afforded us for discussion', said she, 'there was no response; the second time I stayed away. I'd thought about it by this time, and prayed about it—and I had my answer ready: "Lord, I cannot do this. This is not my language, and I am no teacher." Two weeks later a brochure appeared out of the blue, stating the date for the teachers' preparatory class. Straightway, I phoned; but the final answer was: "Oh, you come! We'll teach you, and you'll be able to teach others." That is how I went along.'

Thinking back, Mrs Sliedrecht was able to add, 'The course lasted five days, and was attended by four Africans and three Europeans. And even if I had never used what I learned then, I would not have missed those five days for anything. Such a challenge! There was Mrs Ngcobo—whose husband was a minister in Zululand—sixty, and wanting to teach her own people to read the Bible. Marjorie Shondy was a teacher wanting to teach adults at night. Otty Nxumalo had paid for the course (R.15) and used part of his holiday. Another

was a male nurse, wanting to teach a patient. These
were a sample of the interesting company—and it was
a time of rich fellowship, where bridges were laid, and
the presence of our living Lord felt.'

Literacy is not, of course, merely the power to read
more and more books—but the power to reach a richer
life in a great many ways. Traditionally, women are less
privileged in this respect than men. In Pakistan, only
nine out of 100 women can read and write, against
twenty-seven men—not to mention the deprived margin
who can do neither. Even what Mrs Sliedrecht's directors
call 'functional literacy' is of some worth—the ability to
read simple newspaper articles, to keep in touch with
happenings. While the literacy standard in South Africa
can be claimed to be higher than anywhere else on that
continent, there remains little room for complacency. In
its most developed area—Witwatersrand—thirty-eight
per cent of the non-European population is illiterate;
and the position is worse in many rural parts.

For some months at the start, Mrs Sliedrecht found
herself wondering whether she was wasting her time; and
that of her husband, who undertook to take and fetch
her. And she was still wondering, when she met one of
the husbands in the supermarket. 'Mrs Sliedrecht', said
he, 'you do not know what you have done for my
wife. She is a different person.' 'He took my hand, to
tell me this', said Mrs Sliedrecht to me. Then she added,
encouraged, 'Last week I met the father of Sarah and
Naomi. "You have given my daughters their self-
respect back," said he. And I think', added she, 'of how
I nearly didn't start. And now I feel humble that God
can use the little knowledge I have. They are great
people, these! One is a grandfather, but he is making
good progress. Most have a way to go; but besides
the learning, we all enjoy the fellowship threaded with
laughter. There has developed a bond that I wouldn't
have missed for anything in the world!'

MY PRAYER
Before ever anyone spoke a word, O Lord, much less
wrote it for others to read, your word went forth: 'Let
there be light!' And there was light.

I rejoice that in the ages since, you have never ceased
to speak that commanding word—in the place of ignorance, of cruelty, of superstition—and light has come.

I marvel that in Jesus, your Son, light has been per-
sonified—its rightness and loveliness seen and known
on earth. Forgive me that ever I have been slow to walk
in his way.

Forgive me for my ignorance—self-chosen, in the face
of light; for my casualness, my carelessness, my doubts.
Let the power to read and write serve my liberation.

Save me from knowing the truth—and failing to live
it; for walking in pride, instead of eager humility; from
being content, whilst others lack what I have to share.

Save me, O God, from offering my skills—instead of
myself, in love;

from spending my energies only in what will bring
public acclaim;

from any sense of independence in this life I ought
to share.

Grant that I may never disown the poor, the dull, the
uninteresting, the needy; or bend my knees to the in-
solent, the powerful. Give me grace to walk gladly, and
eagerly in the earth. AMEN

OUR PRAYER TOGETHER
O God, we have much joy and interest in the books we
have read—linking us with lovely minds, and adventurous spirits.

Books and pictures have pushed out our horizons. We
have got to know many splendid people we might not
have known otherwise.

Bless, we pray, all who spend their working lives
writing, editing, publishing and distributing good books,

good journals, good papers.

Bless especially all who devote their energies to the translation of the Bible into modern versions—and all who make them available cheaply, by their gifts of money and loving concern. A M E N

STARTING WITH ORANGE-TREES

Headlines of strife so often arrest the on-going pattern of our days. But they seem the more tragic for coming, as some do, in the Christmas season. It was in that season of goodwill that, in 1963, fierce fighting broke out between Greek and Turkish Cypriots.

Bad news travels swiftly, good news often with laggard feet, it seems. So I have had to wait till lately to hear of the orange-trees. For that very reason I've been glad to have Anne Musgrave's letter—winged to my letter-box with bright stamps from Cyprus. An Irish Presbyterian, in her middle twenties, she deals with retarded children—the only speech-therapist on the island, as far as she knows, outside the British sovereign base area. A day later the post brought me a photograph from Roy Calvocoressi, who, despite my difficulty in pronouncing his name, is an English barrister. Also in their team, whose aim is to actualize Christian methods of peace-making, is Michael Kennedy who, after a modest start with the orange-trees, has moved on to Kidasi; Allan Logie, a young Canadian mechanical engineer; and Michel Bousseri, a French Catholic priest.

In a way, the whole adventure started when the scraggy orange-trees—abandoned during the time of strife and fierce suspicion—touched off the neighbourly concern of the new-comers. The trees' owners were afraid to expose themselves.

After eighteen months of care, the trees were plainly in much better shape; and a new spirit of goodwill had been introduced into the community. The team—under Roy Calvocoressi as co-ordinator—calls itself CHIPS, short for Christian International Peace-making Service.

By now, the team—moving on to other practical tasks —has proved that there can be no hope of the peace of which the Christmas season sings unless, individually and collectively, they learn to acknowledge the wholeness of it—'*Glory to God in the highest, peace on earth to men of goodwill.*' They belong together—one flowing out of the other. So they seek to give 'glory to God' *first* in all their undertakings. They are not peace-hopers, peace-eulogizers. They have no expectation that peace will 'just come'. They do not confuse our Lord's words: 'Blessed are the peacemakers, for they shall be called sons of God' (Matthew 5:9). They do not put the emphasis on the word 'peace', but on the 'makers'. Peace, they see, is not alone a cessation of hostilities, so much as the prosecution of the good, fair, full life, which is God's will for his people on earth.

A group of so-called 'foreigners', whatever they do, may well fall under suspicion from both sides: Are they from America's Central Intelligence Agency? On the other hand, might they not be Communist spies? Only by sincere, practical links with individuals and families, reaching out over twenty-and-more villages, can the faint hope that began with the orange-trees be built into a reliable relationship. The Greek Cypriot Government, together with the Turkish Cypriot community, now at last provide most of the resources. But it all hinges on personnel—self-giving, Christian personnel. A day of wonder dawned for the peace-makers when the Turkish Cypriot side sank a new bore for irrigation, and the Greek Cypriot District Officer applied for a permit to connect the system of distribution to the pump-houses.

Peace does not appear overnight; it has to be *made*!

MY PRAYER

O living Lord, we bow in this silence—that we might know ourselves the better;

that we might know our 'neighbours'—not only those near geographically, but those afar, bound with us;

and that we might the better know you—source of all true justice, compassion and practical aid.

Our war-torn world needs peace so desperately—
where there is friction, grant us a new reasonableness;
where there is suspicion, a new toleration and trust;
where hard work is called for, strong hands and stout
hearts.

We do not for one moment believe, as we pray, that
we must overcome your divine reluctance—rather that
we must find ways of laying hold of your highest willing-
ness.

Lest this prayer degenerate into vague, general terms,
I hush my heart in your presence. Show me what to do
—and how to do it in the manner of Christ, the Prince
of Peace. A M E N

OUR PRAYER TOGETHER
In every age, men and women have heard the accents of
your voice—
    in the mysterious sounds of winds and rains,
    in the thundering might of seas,
    in the fruitfulness of grass and garden,
    in the dependence of childhood, and the frailty of
        old age,
    in laughter and hard work, in sickness and death,
    in fear and hunger and human need of bread;
    in the hour of wonder, and the moment of ecstasy,
    in the misery of war, and in the search for peace.
Speak to us, O Lord, in this place where we find ourselves—that we go from here other than we were when
we came here to keep silence.

Take our ambitions, our skills, our relationships, our
energies;
and use them in this modern century to build peace. For
Christ's sake. A M E N

THE DOCTOR
WHO NEVER STANDS UP

Among the girls growing up in the Syrian Christian community of Kerala, Mary Verghese stood out. Her beautiful wide dark eyes, and smile, saw to that. Some of her young friends were still puzzled about what they wanted to be—but not Mary. She looked at her hands, when she thought herself unobserved; as a Christian girl, she wanted to use them for God.

She enrolled as a student at Vellore, the famous medical college founded by Dr Ida Scudder. Towards the end of 1940, Mary began training. The chapel was the centre of Vellore life; students and patients alike from many religious backgrounds were aware of that. Young Christians, like Mary, believed that the Divine Healer himself walked the corridors.

After training, she was happy to stay on, to qualify still further in surgery. Dr Paul Brand, the already famous surgeon, she knew would teach her how to use her hands. And there were scattered villages for miles around where students and doctors went regularly to hold clinics. Mary longed to be able to help cure illnesses and deformities in the twisted bodies of little children, and grown-ups, and send them back smiling into life. But how could she guess what it would cost her to do it?

On one of the village trips, the station-wagon in which Mary and others were travelling all but collided with a bullock-cart, swerved into the deep dust, hit a mile-stone and, with a grinding of metal, turned over at the bottom of a bank. All were shaken; Dr Mary terribly hurt—but to what extent, it was not at once plain. Her face was gashed, her cheek-bone and clavicle broken. Only after she had laid several days unconscious in hos-

pital was it known that she was paralysed from the
waist down. Doctors and nurses fought for her life.
Some found themselves feeling it would be more merci-
ful could she die. Her spine was broken.

In due time, Dr Paul Brand performed two fusion
operations on her spine, which, together with a cor-
dectomy to relieve pain and spasm, kept her helpless
for many agonizing months. It was no easy task to
break to Dr Mary, so devoted to her work, the serious-
ness of her case—but it was impossible to keep it from
her. She had to face the fact that she would never again
walk the wards of the hospital. But her spine, re-
fashioned, to be one solid column from the head down,
made it possible for her to accept a sitting position in a
wheel-chair. It required rare courage—but it was Christian courage, and enough. To the doctor, sitting a
moment on the side of her bed one day, Mary said a
surprising thing: 'I believe that God is going to bring
me into full medical work again . . . to work with leprosy patients.' *He has*!

Her hands and arms uninjured, she has learned to sit
in her wheel-chair, and get herself around. All the
delicate operations that can be done sitting down—to
faces, hands, feet—Dr Mary has mastered. 'I can tell
you now', says Dr Paul Brand, 'that she is one of the
most skilful hand surgeons in the East . . . She is in
charge of the leprosy ward; she does out-patient clinics
. . . and she is working a full day every day of the week.
. . . The thing that shines through her is her faith—the
faith that made her know from the beginning that God
had a work for her to do.' Speaking of her leprosy
patients, he adds, wonderingly: 'I can see them sometimes in their despondency, in their despair, in their
apathy—and then I see Mary coming, working her
wheel-chair without any assistance from anybody. She
still has the scar across her face where it was once cut
open, but as she comes round the corner, I see a light,
a new light, come on to the faces of those leprosy

patients. I believe it's a heavenly light.'
It is!

MY PRAYER

I do not look now for a halo to mark out those who serve you—but I know the signs.

I give thanks especially today for all who train and minister through the on-going medium of medicine and surgery.

I seek your blessing on all who train students, all who work behind the scenes in labs, in kitchens, laundries, supply-rooms.

I seek your blessing on all patients who are young; all hurt through accidents of any kind.

I seek your presence with all who find patience taxed during their long stay in hospital.

I pray for any who have to battle with hopelessness, with depression, and go out to unhelpful home settings.

I pray especially for those who lack a lively faith—who feel that they are facing their hurdles alone.

Challenge more with good gifts of compassion, health and strength,

I pray, to continue Christ's ministry to the sick today,

You know me so much better than I know myself, O Lord—

> 'Direct, control, suggest this day
> All I design, or do, or say;
> That all my powers, with all their might,
> To thy sole glory may unite.' AMEN

OUR PRAYER TOGETHER

Lord, keep us sensitive to the needs of others—needs of body, mind and spirit;

Lord, keep us responsive to your call—in love, adoration, praise;

Lord, use our splendid energies—in the work we do; in the community where we move; in the home where we live.

There is no good and lovely thing for any of us, but comes from you—

So our first and last act together here would be to utter praise and thanksgiving. Hear us, we pray. A M E N

FRIEDAL PETER

As far back as anyone could remember, life had gone on the same in Esmatabad. Then suddenly, in the night of 1 September 1962, at 10.52 p.m., the earth split—and nothing was ever the same again.

Those who had taken their pallets up on to the flat roofs that hot night fared better than others. The last thing they saw before sleep came was the watching moon—between the slim silver of newness and the stronger crescent of first quarter. And the thing that met them immediately on waking was a world in ruins. Anguished cries rose from many of those who had made their beds indoors—countless others were crushed to silence beneath the weight of broken houses.

In newspaper-offices the world round, men and women who had never so much as heard of Esmatabad set to spell out its tragic name. A major earthquake of such dimensions made headlines, temporarily at any rate. For the stricken it was another story. With winter's rain and snow only a week or so away, many who had escaped would likely find themselves threatened with exposure—already the death-toll stood at eleven thousand, and twenty thousand were homeless.

But to Friedal Peter—a Swiss Moravian—every group of statistics had faces. He approached all need, as his Master Christ had done always, in terms of people. From serving as an engineer in needy Pakistan, now he was summoned by Inter-Church Aid to oversee its relief plan in Esmatabad. Immediate help was forthcoming, but it was plain that long-term planning would be required. The Government of Iran set its mind to the matter—and agreed that it seemed only sensible to plan to replace the little mud crofts that had long been the centre of family life with something better—with buildings known to be earthquake-proof. The Government decided on a steel-ribbed design—other parts of the country had already tested them over ten years; there was experience to draw on. If the buildings could not be so picturesque, they would be safer.

Work went ahead. At the end of two crowded years, the World Council of Churches had fulfilled its compassionate undertaking. Other agencies did their share— Esmatabad was a team task, Christian and Muslim. Following the extreme heat of summer, it was hardly to be expected that a casual onlooker would visualize peasant people in raggedly worn clothes facing winter—a charcoal bowl beneath each family table the only warmth. Friedal Peter set his heart on providing something both safer and more adequate. There was need, too, for clinics, communal laundries, bath-houses, shops, schools and, above all, a clean water supply. Old Esmatabad had drawn its water from a doubtful, sluggish source. And since Inter-Church Aid set out to *aid* people—not to bribe them into becoming Christians—room on the plan was left for a new mosque, to be paid for eventually by a helpful Muslim Foundation.

But how seldom life works out as simply as on the drawing-board! Oddly, many locals preferred the illiteracy they knew to the lessons the school provided—letting the young boys go to the fields and the girls go on bearing the babies. Esmatabad—for all the Aid—did not become a success-story overnight.

But Friedal Peter has not failed—for he possesses a lively patience with people—a Christian patience!

MY PRAYER

O Lord, I want never to take my good night's rest for granted—

   the safety of my home;
   the refreshment and strength it spells;
   nor the love and loyalty of those who share it.

I want to keep wide open with a welcome, both the door
of my heart
    and of my home—
    for neighbours and friends;
    for the lonely, the perplexed;
    for the foolish, and the unfortunate.
Show me how to lighten a sorrowful heart;
    to set peace upon a lined brow;
    to start a smile on a drawn face;
    to be the means of your guidance, your building up.
Let me not miss my chance to do some of these wonderful things—through gazing afar, or lamenting my own
limited gifts;
  let no unfeeling moment, or over-busyness, find me
unready; support me all the day long, and into the
night. For Christ's sake. AMEN

OUR PRAYER TOGETHER
O God, you have set us to live in this modern world,
concerned for each other's safety;
able to rise above differences of race;
    of religion;
    of political ideology.
eager to share skills, money and possessions,
    during natural disasters;
    in poverty, sickness, and war.
Bestir us here and now to make relief instant and adequate;
    to help build up the broken;
    to beautify the dull and ugly.
Bless with strength and health all who serve our fellows—
    in trying climates;
    with small resources.
Keep alive in us your patience, your encouragement—
and let us know, if it is your will, the satisfaction of
your true workers and builders. In the name of Christ.
                                      AMEN

AN ARTIST, SIR!

The neighbours stepped in to see the new baby; but none really knew what to say. Voice after voice betrayed a note of pity. Wee John, born into their midst in Glasgow, was without proper hands—just stumps, with two partly-formed fingers.

John's father found life already something of a hurdle. He was an old soldier—with one leg. He worked, when he was able, in a Government air factory; and sometimes as a labourer. But it was not easy to get suitable jobs, and there were anxious intervals of unemployment. The mother of the family did what she could—filling in with work off and on at a laundry near home. The wee fellow's future seemed dark indeed. How could anyone envision a day when he would have his work in a great cathedral, and enjoy the patronage of a queen?

When he was old enough, the lad came under the care of the National Children's Home. It took him a little time to settle happily in the branch for crippled children at Chipping Norton, in the beautiful Cotswold countryside. It was his good fortune to be in the kindly care of Sister Adela Fordham. All that love-inspired imagination and experience could do, she and her colleagues did for John.

Eager—as courage developed—to do all that other boys did, he became a Boy Scout. And all went well, until he was required to do his 'tenderfoot test', part of which called for the tying of a number of knots. How could a boy with John's handicap tie knots? His Scoutmaster saw the situation, and whispered that in his case one would do. But John's answer was instant, and with no uncertainty: 'No fear! I won't take the badge if I can't do the lot!' And facing up to them in his own way, he managed them.

When it came time to settle on some further training for a career, John was asked, like all the others, what he had in mind. 'I want to be an artist, sir', said he. 'But could you be an artist, without hands?' came the rather daunting query, realistic as life had to be. 'I want to, sir', was John's reply. And in time, he made his way to the Oxford School of Art—on a scholarship. The registrar, when he looked up as the new student was shown in, asked with surprise, 'But haven't you come to the wrong school? We teach art here.' 'No, sir,' came the modest answer, 'I have a scholarship!'

John Buchanan's rare gifts lay in illumination—in perfection of lettering, design and sense of colour.

With experience, he was able to establish his own studio. This was a great satisfaction; not least, that he found himself honoured with orders from the Queen, and members of the Royal Household. Those responsible also sought out an example of his lovely work for the Liverpool Cathedral. And printed collections and calendars bearing his name—turned out by budding craftsmen at the National Children's Home works— made their appearance in many parts of the world.

John's letter to me—when I asked if I might tell his story in a series I was doing on Christian courage—is one I will always keep. 'I deeply regret,' he wrote modestly, 'that I am no example of Christian courage, having only tried to earn a living with a deformed body. Also, as I have known no other way of managing, it is not so hard for me as for the poor fellows deprived of limbs in later life. But do as you wish, only don't make it too remarkable—mainly it has been patience and continuous effort which the good God has rewarded.' *But isn't this Christian courage?*

The National Children's Home still cares for over three thousand girls and boys—as individuals.

MY PRAYER

Gracious Lord, daily I rise, to wash, to dress, to eat═
to live and move in the strength of my body;
> in the light of my mind;
> in the mysterious energy of my will.

Daily I find the hours filled with friendly associations,
as I move freely in my home;
> in my place of work;
> in my leisure pursuits.

I cannot pretend that every person about me
> is as happily situated;
> is as physically and mentally fit;
> is as free to come and go.

I cannot pretend that every person about me
never accepting these good gifts
> as mine of right;
> by favouritism;
> by smart family management.

Bless this day all for whom every day is another battle;
> a day of rare courage;
> a day of faith;
> a day of specialized service.

Bless all who, against such odds, make of life a splendid,
triumphant thing. AMEN

OUR PRAYER TOGETHER

O God, you have made this world a very wonderful
place═with the endless shape, and colour, and feel of
things;

You have given us the mighty mountains, and seas,
and rivers, and the flowers, more gloriously arrayed
than Solomon;

You have placed within our human choice issues
whose ends reach out beyond here and now;

You have fashioned us for worship, and work, and
loving care, and made it possible for us to move about
freely.

Save, we pray, all who carry daily burdens we do not
    know;
Encourage, we pray, the handicapped in body, or
    mind;
And support all who offer to their fellows new oppor-
    tunities.
If we in turn have hard things to do, sustain us in good
spirit, and bring us to our beds each night without
shame or self-pity.
    And to your great name be all the praise and glory.
                                                    A M E N

A WELCOME OVER THE DOOR-STEP

Our Lord was a man often without a roof over his head. In the warm climate of Palestine—though nights there, I found, could be cold—this mightn't have been such a tragedy. But in London, in modern times, it could amount to that. Thanks to Hilda Porter, M.B.E., 'Auntie Hilda' to countless people of all nations, a brighter story can be told.

On 11 August 1950, Miss Porter and a friend or two ready to tackle the colossal task, moved into a large, dilapidated building in Inverness Terrace—to be called, by the time I knew it, 'M.I.H.', Methodist International House. Scrubbing-brushes and screwdrivers were still the order of those days, and Hilda had tramped London's streets to find this house. The price the agents set was £27,000—a lot of money, when money was short. But Hilda was not a large-hearted Yorkshire-woman for nothing. Also, she had had early experience in business under her father, the managing-director of a textile engineering firm; training in Kingsmead College; followed by a year's practical medicine; and a year's language-study in Wuchang, before a first appointment in a bandit-infested area in Central China. 'If the bandits get hold of Hilda Porter,' her supervisor, Dr H. B. Rattenbury, had said, 'they'll deserve all they get.'

The political unrest sent her home; but eighteen years later—more determined, more experienced—she was back again. In the meantime, her sister had died; her father had called again on her help in business; through the Mission House in London, she had undertaken an organizing appointment covering much of Britain; and when the blitz started, and bombs fell on civilians, she had found work with the hundreds who, each night in

Rivercourt Methodist Hall, lay down in rows to sleep as best they could. Hilda already knew what it meant to 'sleep rough'. To this day she shows a crowned front tooth, harking back to a night when, travelling in China through thirteen of the eighteen provinces, she made her bed amid a pile of rice-sacks aboard a boat, and a sleeping man from above fell—to find his elbow in an English woman's mouth.

In that very London in which M.I.H. was to be so welcome, Hilda had visited and, more recently, been visited by, coloured students living in a bleak one-time fire-watching station near her home—miserable, homesick, lonely. They, too, had tramped the streets of the metropolis—knocked on doors—but when landladies had seen their skin-colour, had found doors slammed abruptly. Hilda did what she could personally; but she longed to mobilize the Church. It was not easy. But at last a day came when the Mission treasurer said to her, 'Go and get your hotel!' She met the agents, brought them down to half their price; and later secured the property's freehold as well. With her helpers—following that August day of scrubbing and shining—they prepared a room a day, to be immediately occupied. The first student to enter came from Nigeria —now Dr O. K. Ogan, one of the most highly qualified gynaecologists in that needy country. Already by the time I knew M.I.H., representatives of eighty-two countries had shared its hospitable roof. Extensions were the order of the day, and the setting up of a small chapel. It fell to me to enjoy the privilege of presenting its first Bible. And what I chose to inscribe on its fly-leaf might as fittingly have been written over all life at M.I.H. '*To the Glory of God, our Father*!'

'If we believe that all people are God's children,' Hilda Porter said plainly, 'then we must live that way.' M.I.H. has proved only the first in a growing vision reaching to many cities. Its founder—retired now—has abundantly proved herself 'a friend of all the Family'.

MY PRAYER

I thank you, eternal Father, for a glimpse of a day when all members of your world-family—of whatever colour and clime—will live together in peace and dignity, serving you with devotion.

I thank you for any who have glimpsed the fringes of this dream, and, here and now, tied it to reality, in the name of Christ. For all who have been undaunted by the ever-present difficulties.

Grant that I may never fail you in offering an open door, open heart—and sincere respect for human personality. Let me not forget how Christ wore human nature, to your glory.

Teach me the stewardship of my share of the manifold resources of the earth—that fewer may know surfeit whilst many faint with need. In work and play, let me learn how to share.

Near at hand, and known to me, are societies with hands outreached to help; let me not resent their appeals. They seem to come so often—and must, till need is met.

So many, through the years, have offered me help, that now my conscience stirs at remembrance of Christ's words: 'Unto whosoever much is given, of him shall be much required.' You know the measure of my sincerity in this human matter. AMEN

OUR PRAYER TOGETHER

Father, accept our worship—our praise and thanksgiving —both spoken and offered in silence.

We open our secret hearts to you who are wholly to be trusted—we own our sins, our human stupidities.

Lacking the strength and spirit to carry through our dreams, we look to you for help.

We do not ask for anything that is not for our good,

and that of our fellows, in this wonderful but challenging world.

Deliver us from superiority, from social snobbishness, from self-absorption. In these days of confusion, teach us how to live.

Let thy Kingdom come—and thy good will be done!

AMEN

GIANT SMALL MAN

Young William Merrell Vories, small of stature, managed to dodge those who would disturb his conscience. And this wasn't easy. His family often entertained world travellers whose talk at table was of needy folk. At Colorado College, too, his best friends belonged to the Student Christian Movement. But with a little cunning he managed to shrug off thoughts that service of the sort they talked about was anything to do with him. 'I'm going to be an architect,' he would answer when things got awkward, 'and make a lot of money. Then,' he would add with a chuckle, 'I can support half a dozen missionaries.'

For a time things stayed that way. Then, one day he startled his family with an announcement: 'It's come, my dream job!' Through the Y.M.C.A. he had learned that a man was needed in Omi-Hachiman. It was somewhere in the hinterland of Japan, it seemed, and sounded rather fun. Young William straightway borrowed from his father enough for the ticket money.

Reaching Tokyo, he learned a little more of the place he was off to—a stronghold of fanatical Buddhism. One man, he had to admit, had a poor chance of making much of a dint. But life still had surprises in store for him.

The first night—after a trying seventeen-hour train trip—an earthquake suddenly rattled the walls of the little house where he sought sleep. When it ceased, he took up his diary, and wrote, 'Homesick, cold, lonely. *But here!*'

Next day, he set about his class-work. And in a little time, had made a few friends. He invited the boys to his house, played dominoes with them, and served supper.

He went to the length of promising Bible Study, expecting about six to turn up. Forty-five arrived. At what he judged the moment, he flipped over his large blackboard, and used it flat as a ping-pong board.

When several of his boys, months on, became Christians, he invited them to share his crazy little house. Soon they were joined by eight of the academy's brightest. They needed badly a Y.M.C.A. of their own. After a search, a Christian dairyman gave land; thirty of William's friends back home sent money; and they got a building up. But suspicious Buddhist priests incited rough students to tackle those who attended. Added to that, by the end of the year, the authorities were prevailed upon to cut off Vories's contract to teach.

Jobless, he reviewed his special training, and started an architectural firm. His first student-draftsman was actually one of his own class-boys, who had come out of a notorious brothel owned by an uncle. Together they set about developing and erecting a new kind of building that would absorb shock on earthquaky sites.

'Isn't this just like God,' exclaimed Vories brightly. 'He asks one to give up a selfish ambition—then he gives it back, saying, "Use it for me!"' So the Omi Brotherhood came into being, and a glorious and exact truth got into circulation: *'We're not just building structures—we're building men*!' The brotherhood of builders was not alone an argument for Christianity— it was a demonstration.

By 1948, it had branches in Tokyo, in Osaka, Seoul, Mukden, and Peking. And today, among thousands of buildings it has erected in Japan alone, is the famous Daimaru department-store in Osaka, which I have visited. It cost over ten million dollars and covers a whole block. Also, the Omi Brotherhood now operates a thirty-seven-building T.B. sanatorium, and a Christian educational centre for children of all ages from kindergarten to senior high school. So the building goes on—

the building that is more than bricks and planks!

MY PRAYER

Master Builder, I marvel that you have fashioned this
world so strongly, so beautifully—
> dividing the darkness from the light;
> quickening continually the fertility of the soil;
> setting the stars above, and seas and streams be-
> neath.

I thank you for the shape and feel of things well made—
> for hills and valleys;
> for the limbs of little children;
> for the love of men and women, making homes to-
> gether.

You have shown me the importance of human lives,
human personalities—
> more even than the productiveness of fields;
> grace of brick and beam;
> and exchange of coin in the market-place.

Often I have hammered away so loudly that I have not
heard you speak—nor even cared if you had a plan for
me.

Forgive me, and bring me again to good sense; that,
shedding my pride, I may serve you with joy.

So may I have your blessing, great Master Builder.

AMEN

OUR PRAYER TOGETHER

Number us, O Lord of life, among those of the earth
who build up rather than smash down.

Of childhood, we have seen, can be fashioned a
delicate growth of promise;

Of youth, can be made a heaven or a hell, a character
to rejoice in, or lament.

Help us to handle these everlasting materials, and
build aright—
> showing patience to little children;

appreciating youth's point of view;

co-operating with all set on the Kingdom of Christ. So may we bridge the 'gap' between ourselves—and between us and your great self, O God. In the name of the Carpenter of Nazareth. A M E N

KEEP WORKING AT IT, SON!

Glenn and Floyd Cunningham loved the old farm home in Cimarron Valley. There were always interests to share. And a morning came when they could hardly wait to eat breakfast. It was their turn to light the school stove, and they wanted to get it done quickly. It was a crisp, cold morning. 'Come on,' called Glenn, 'we'll be late!' Next moment, having caught up his bag, Floyd was following.

With their cheeks freshened by the run, the two boys tackled the old stove. It had its moods—some mornings it was very stubborn to start. But Floyd felt sure they could get it going; he knew where there was a can of petroleum. And he brought it out and poured it over the wood in the stove.

But it was not petroleum—and the instant the match met it, it went up in a mighty blaze, blotting out everything in a sheet of flame. It was petrol.

When friends in the playground heard the cry, they came to the rescue. With coats and old sacks, they beat back the flames. Glenn was so badly burned that it seemed certain he would never run again—and he so loved to run! In no time, Dr Harvey Hansen was on the scene, and at sight of Glenn a great tenderness came into his voice, and a doubt into his mind that Glenn would even be able to walk again. Laughter died out of the playground that day, as they carried Glenn home.

For weeks and weeks he lay in his bed, unable to move. His schoolfriends crept in on tip-toe from time to time. Then, little by little, Glenn found that he could move his poor burned legs. But he might never have managed more had his mother not come forward with the right word: 'The Lord made you whole, and he wants you whole now . . .' And with that, she massaged

Glenn's legs. When she had to stop to get a meal, or to do some homely chore, she set him to continue the massaging himself. 'Keep working at it, son,' she would say. And he did! He managed, in time, to get out of bed; six months later he was taking his first uneasy steps. That was a great day. It took courage, but always his mother's words echoed in his ears: 'Keep working at it, son!' The time came when he could lean his whole weight on the handles of the plough, and follow with his feet in the furrow. Soon, a limp was the only outward reminder of his accident. And the old desire to run rose again in his heart. Without saying anything to anyone, he put his name down for a school-boy race—and won! When he got home, his mother smiled. 'Just keep working at it, son' was all she said. And the day came when the cheers of his friends reached the skies as the young athlete roared home!

In 1952—a student at the University of Kansas—Glenn was chosen to represent his State at the Olympics. Again the chorus reached the skies! Two years later, Glenn was bettering his own shining record. 'The Iron Man' they called him, such was his endurance. An outstanding student, soon, at the University of New York, Glenn found himself surrounded by many friends—and some enemies. His friends were the wholesome, bracing things of life—his enemies, those that spoil a fellow's fitness. 'I have known athletes who use alcoholic beverages,' said he, 'but they don't last!'

To hold the world's record in the mile run was fine—but not enough for Glenn. He saved money, he married. And after World War II, when most people expected him to return to teaching at Cornell College, where he had earned his doctorate in physical education, he got himself a ranch and a herd of cattle.

Life—from many stories reaching him—is plainly tough for a number of youngsters. 'Juvenile delinquents' they are labelled. Glenn and his wife Ruth now use their ranch-home for these. 'When the larder is near empty, and bills overdue,' he says, 'I go afield to get help, lecturing. Ruth goes to prayer. We try to strengthen personal faith through religious services, plus heavy doses of love.

'And often, I have occasion to pass on to a half-beaten boy *my mother's words*!'

MY PRAYER
O God, my Father, I thank you for all who live well, and love much;

I thank you for my own home—and for all happy homes and their supporting background;

I thank you for good gifts of character handed on, and unfailingly shared.

I seek your guidance for all who engage in sport— players and participants in any way;

Grant that standards set may be of the highest—and that bodies as well as minds and spirits may praise you. AMEN

OUR PRAYER TOGETHER
O God, we rejoice in our physical fitness—received, and developed;

in the companionship of family, and friends—in goals set, and achieved.

Enable us to keep these gifts unspoiled—against the erosion of lower standards,

against dishonest haste, monetary gain above all—as time wears on.

Keep us considerate of professionals, who face temptations few of us know.

So may we together set out eagerly—and come home unashamed.

In the name of Christ, our Lord. AMEN

MORE THAN WITCHCRAFT

Wearing her tall hat, from time beyond time, the old witch still rides her broomstick about the world. Countless story-books show her; though few, if any, story-loving children accept her means of travel as a reality.

Has anyone suggested to Annie Vallotton, in her childhood home in Switzerland, that she would one day as easily ride about the world on a pencil, she would have laughed at the idea. Yet this has happened!

If you have acquired a paperback in the best-selling list—*Good News for Modern Man*, sub-titled, *The New Testament in Today's English Version*—you will not call it incredible.

The Vallotton family was a clutch of lively book-lovers—and missionary minded. A friendship with Dr Albert Schweitzer—missionary and musician extraordinary—was rich and real. Annie's father, Benjamin, became widely known for his distinguished writings and lectures; as in time did her brother Pierre, a minister of the Protestant church in Saint-Dié, not only for his preaching, but also for the church's magnificent organ, the work of his hands. A gifted family!

Annie's first interest was the violin; but persistent cramp in one of her thumbs during her late teens, brought this dream to an end. Whether she could have circled the earth on a violin bow is in doubt; but nobody now doubts her ability to do it on a pencil!

She acquired her training in design at the Ecole des Arts Décoratifs in Strasbourg. The time came when she set about illustrating children's books and Bible songs, writing books herself, and appearing on special TV programmes in Geneva—narrating a story, and drawing for it at the same time. It has been my joy to talk with her.

But it is her lively little New Testament sketches that have put the whole world in her debt. She can't remember a time when she didn't love those stories. Long before the idea was at all general that they should be published in a format as attractive as any other book, and left around, Annie was expounding this idea.

Adult, and by this time much experienced in things artistic—Mlle Vallotton began selecting suitable verses from her beloved New Testament to illustrate with her striking outline drawings. She has evolved delightful little figures without facial features, with which each of us can identify, irrespective of age or race. And this is a real part of their fascination. So clear are they that anyone can appreciate them, so animated that the stories they illustrate come alive in a new way—and they are not without a sense of humour, alongside deep insight. No matter how many other modern translations of the New Testament are to hand, Mlle Annie Vallotton—riding our world from country to country on her enchanted pencil—has given us each a lively experience! With her dedicated help, words from the brief Preface of *Good News for Modern Man* have become acknowledged truth: 'The New Testament does not merely inform; it demands decision and calls for commitment on the part of those who read this Good News.'

MY PRAYER
Gracious Lord, I praise you as the source of all good things—

> not least, your message that has come to me through scribes, scholars and translators;
> not least, your message now closely related to my life through teachers, preachers and illustrators.

Grant me a freshness of approach, as I turn its pages, and

> a thoughtful eagerness, and memory for what I learn,
> that my daily life may take on a new dimension,

and my response to you be more intelligent and
Christ-like.
Bless all the great Bible Societies making this book
available
in the world, where so many of us need continual
guidance, instruction and support;
where so many other voices clamour to be heard—
speak to my heart, and let me embrace your truth.
I pray especially for all reading the New Testament for
the first time—in the name of the living Christ, today
and forever. AMEN

OUR PRAYER TOGETHER
Almighty God, we marvel that from the beginning of
time, men and women have acknowledged responsibility for the use of the gifts you have granted them—
Moses, with his rod, when you asked, 'What is that
in thine hand?'
David with his harp of enchanting music, and voice
of song;
Nehemiah, and his men with their bricks and building trowels;
Mary, the village maiden, with her capacity for
motherhood;
Dorcas, with her needle-and-thread, and cutting,
sewing skill;
Priscilla, with her wifely skills, and ever-open door.
We rejoice that you still accept our several gifts in your
holy service, on-going in this world today. AMEN

The door kept opening. More and more women silently filled the seats in the little waiting-room. Some immediately joined in turning over magazines—the usual array of out-dated and dog-eared. But fresh copies were there, too, and a few humorous ones. On the wall opposite was a fine etching of the Cathedral in Prague; next, a coloured print; and for some who could see from where they sat, two or three more as unexpected in a doctor's waiting-room.

But this was Dr Marion Hilliard's waiting-room—and everybody in Toronto was prepared for the unexpected where their beloved doctor was concerned. Brilliant Chief of Obstetrics and Gynaecology of the Woman's College Hospital, she was an acknowledged pioneer. Hers was the first general hospital in Canada founded, staffed and administered entirely by women. And Dr Marion Hilliard had made it famous the world round. Patients to her were always people first. Some—like those around the walls of the waiting-room—were there because of pain; others because of secret fears; all, to consult another woman whom they could trust. She was lovely to look at, lively, human, above all, Christian.

Nurtured by parents who believed in her as she grew, little Marion was 'in love with life' from the start—free to adventure, free to serve. There were four others in the small-town family: Foster, Ruth, Helen and Irwin. Father was an established lawyer—his threefold interests, home, church and community. Mrs Hilliard's days were as full whatever the season, though each of the children had home tasks. All learned music. And, lessons finished, there was always the horse, and the cow, and the chickens, and fun in the hay-loft! Nobody could remember a time when Marion was not an enthusiastic leader.

She carried it over into early college days. Teachers found her easy to teach—a good student. At eighteen— suitcase in hand—she set off for the great city, or so Toronto seemed to her. Would she be a teacher? Or make music her career? She entered the honours course in science and biology. And the day came when she broke it to her father that her real dream was to become a doctor.

With her usual eagerness, she got her Bachelor of Arts degree; after three further years of study and practical work, she graduated in medicine. A scholarship then made it possible for her to go to Britain. Some of her internship she served in Ireland. And in all her distinguished career, nothing is more meaningful than an experience belonging to this early time. She related it with a chuckle, little knowing what it spelled out. 'I'll never forget the door-man at the hospital in Dublin,' she would begin. 'Part of his duty was to waken those of us needed to take cases during the night. There were twelve of us—I was the only woman.' But in that team she reached a stage where it was clear to all that she was getting more calls than any of the others. When at last she charged him with it, his reply was simply, 'Oh, I know, Doctor; *but you wake so easy*!'

She re-told it as a joke. But it was more than that. No human need found her unresponsive, no bother was beyond her—she 'waked so easy'. And over the years, she studied, she wrote, she lectured, she diagnosed, she directed—she carried into the multitudinous claims of a great modern hospital the spirit of the Great Physician. And there that spirit persists!

MY PRAYER
O God, I thank you for the gift of health—and, when illness befalls me,

for the wisdom of physicians;
for the skill of surgeons;
for the judgment of anaesthetists;
for the continual support of nurses;
for the loving interest of friends.

I reach out through you, O God, with a new sympathy and concern—

to those I know, possessed by fear;
to those long bed-fast;
to those at last relaxed, and come again to health.

Through us all, in turn, may your best plans for wholeness of body,

mind and spirit be perfected today;
keep us hopeful and co-operative;
and ready to drop the past behind,
and press on eagerly, with lively thanksgiving.

AMEN

OUR PRAYER TOGETHER

O God, it is easy when 'out of sorts' to worry about ourselves—

to worry about an awaited diagnosis;
to worry about the family, and those at work;
to worry about the length of time we must lie in bed.

Deliver us from negative thoughts that go round and round;

from all self-pity that holds no healing;
from lack of co-operation with doctors and nurses;
from discouragement if the first promise of recovery is not sustained.

Let quiet patience enable us to try again,

thankful that every day brings some reminder of your nearness—
books to read, flowers to enjoy, letters from afar—
and that all the time research continues, bringing new light to bear on diseases stubborn to resist.

Preserve in health all who devote their lives to healing—

give them the caring heart, the gentle touch, the
  hopeful voice;
so that the ill and hurt may mend, and the incurable
  know through them the solace that sustains. For
  Christ's sake. A M E N

SWEETNESS AND GOODNESS

Not every one of us can remember Mrs Mackintosh of the ten-pound copper jam-pan. But her sweetness and goodness is not lost in the world we know. Her pan was one of her few wedding presents, and she polished it till it shone like the sun.

When Mrs Mackintosh was not involved in the busyness of the jam season, she made toffees—and good toffees they were, according to her small son. And grown up, a well-known head of business, he still holds to that conviction.

His father, in turn, had expanded his mother's toffee-making. Factories were raised to meet a growing demand. And in time, the small boy, grown with the years, and possessed of a greater experience than those before him could know, was turning out five hundred tons of toffees *a week*!

And the son of Mrs Mackintosh of the sweet tooth and the ten-pound copper jam-pan saw to it that each single toffee wrapper bore her honourable name. When the time came when he was honoured by the Queen— to bear the title of Lord Mackintosh of Halifax—he told of her. It was at a large and unforgettable gathering of friends and business associates. It was a happy occasion —the table beautifully and bountifully set—with many a guest eager to speak of his host's accomplishments. He was lauded as a successful manufacturer, as a collector of items of art, as World President of the Sunday School Association. But when it was his own turn to speak, he had a simple word-picture to add to the evening, a picture that nobody ever forgot. Memories of his mother, and of his wife, he said, added up to the very sweetest things in life to him.

'When my mother died,' he added, 'we found a little

cardboard box. In it were a photo of my father when they first met, which none of us had seen; *the original toffee recipe* in her own handwriting on the page of an exercise-book; and a letter thanking her for her work as a Sunday school teacher. These', he added proudly, 'were evidently her real treasures.'

And his? Well, there was no secret about his answer to that question. A busy man, much sought-after, involved in modern business concerns on a wide scale, he yet made a place in his life for those things of the spirit that kept his mother's character sweet.

Life—even in toffee-making—had grown unimaginably complex. But in it all, and through it all, simple principles of 'goodness and sweetness' persist.

Within the colourful pageant familiar in the Bible of Lord Mackintosh of Halifax, is treasured the story of two others who early found the secret—King Saul and Jonathan. The Bible says simply, 'Saul and Jonathan were *lovely and sweet in their lives*.' (2 Samuel 1:23.)

Among the many whom the Queen has delighted to honour for service, it is pleasant to remember the witness of this man of business, who insists on one thing: *sweeter than toffees, sweeter than success, sweetness of character lasts*!

MY PRAYER

O God, I shall be busy about the many concerns of my home today—

the routine tasks that have always belonged to home-making;

ordinary matters known in the simple home in Nazareth;

preparing meals, providing clothes, earning money.

Take what skills reside in my hands, and use them well;

save me from going about things too solemnly,

forgetful of fun and laughter,

finding no time for others' interest.

Forgive me for lack of vision, of care, of kindness;

forgive me for criticism that is unhelpful;
forgive me for gossip that rejoices in others' faults;
forgive me for mirth shared only at others' expense.
Remind me continually of the world of men and women outside—

With needs much like my own;
with dreams much like my own;
with experiences much like my own.

Let none of my faults of yesterday hold me back from living well today. Lift me above the burden of things that do not really matter. Lighten my sense of responsibility with clear and sensible thought.

So may the wider world be the sweeter for my loyalty and service. For Christ's sake. A M E N

OUR PRAYER TOGETHER

O God, we bring our thanks for daily gifts besides bread—

water in our taps;
clothes and shoes;
and sweets to enjoy.

Beyond strengthening gifts are the tasty things—
cakes and desserts;
spices and essences;
fruits and conserves.

Beyond even these, is the look of things—
bright colours;
exciting shapes and surfaces;
the fascination of new textures.

You have crowded this world with daily interests—
Let us take none of these good gifts for granted;
and use none wastefully, irresponsibly. But as good stewards. A M E N

YOUNG TOM DOOLEY

Dr Tom's days were full of people—colleagues, friends, and Vietnamese people in the midst of mass evacuation. As a junior doctor in the U.S. Navy, a devout Catholic, he unquestioningly loved people, for love of his Lord. But he had never before been so troubled about human need.

When released from the Navy, he knew at once what he must do. Young, and well trained, he was free to serve, and without first thought of reward. 'We can win the friendship of these,' he found himself explaining to any who would listen, 'by getting down on the ground and working beside them, on equal terms, humans to humans, toward goals that they themselves seek.'

So young Dr Tom found his way back to that shocking scene of need—to do just that—to examine their sick, deliver their babies, attend their weddings and funerals, work with their workers, and play and laugh with their children.

'In Laos,' he wrote in one of his letters home, 'I believe we can build a hospital, stock it, and run it; train the personnel to handle it, and turn it over to them in a period of two to four years. In other areas, it might take longer.'

Colleagues, stores and money would be needed in order to get started. But young Dr Tom Dooley was not a man to be balked by difficulties; in his faith was born a lively and splendid confidence, an unending readiness to plan and hope. And to forward his purpose—shared soon with others—he founded MEDICO, Medical International Co-operation Organization. Its purpose was plain, in words as in practical efforts—to take care of needy people in areas where, without it, they had little or no chance of medical aid.

'How long', he was asked, 'will your doctors stay in an area?' His answer was, 'That depends.' He could give no other answer; at that moment MEDICO as a whole was an experiment in compassion. How could anyone tell what the years would declare?

With two volunteers, Dr Tom Dooley set up in Muong Sing, at the foot of a high mountain. Red China lay six miles off; but the envisioned plan was bigger than any disputed frontiers, conflicts, or political wrangles. It was a crusade in Christ's spirit, in terms of people—since, above all, people would always matter most.

Days and nights of continual service by those three dedicated spirits spelled out miracles to the sick about them.

Then, suddenly, the young doctor himself was stricken. Tests showed it to be cancer—'*Malignant melanoma*' the report read, and young Tom Dooley knew only too well its meaning. There was no time to lose, and no time for self-pity. It could hardly have happened at a worse time—the guerillas infiltrating.

Dooley flew back home for surgery. And scarcely had his incisions healed than—his days numbered—he was up and about among those who might be encouraged to support MEDICO—lecturing, speaking on radio, appearing on television; pausing only long enough to receive the Criss Award. Then off back to Laos!

Time proved shorter than promised. Death claimed Dr Tom Dooley's body—but not his valiant spirit. And what he started still lives!

MY PRAYER

O God of mercy, I rejoice with you in all who minister to bodily need—

> doctors and nurses;
> laboratory staff;
> administrators and record-keepers.

I give thanks for all made aware of new areas of disease—

all instant in response;
 all who see beyond nationality, colour, or clime;
 all constant in peace or war.
I thank you for knowledge and tenderness
 that banish fear;
 that bring comfort and hope;
 that spell out brotherhood in more than words.
Even the ghastly, devilish evils of war go down in defeat
 before this kind of life;
 before this real love;
 before this measure of mercy.
In the name of the Good Physician, Christ, uphold us
all. AMEN

OUR PRAYER TOGETHER
Gracious God, grant awareness of your nearness to our
own beloved sick—
 to any who await a doctor's report;
 to any who are cast about with fears;
 to any who must enter hospital for the first time.
Support with your spirit, O God, all who minister to
body and mind—
 all who persevere in tracking down diseases;
 all who shoulder the training of others;
 all who provide ambulances, and administer hospitals.
Hold in your daily and nightly ministry of renewal
 the fearful, the frail, the bed-ridden;
 the blind, moving in the darkness;
 the deaf, shut out from familiar voices.
And bless especially all concerned relations, chaplains
and almoners—this hour, and forever.
And be pleased to receive from those of us in health,
unending gratitude for what we enjoy. AMEN

WITH THE BREATH OF LIFE

One of a thousand—Medea, Beatrice, Lady Macbeth, Queen Katherine, Saint Joan, not forgetting Miss Moffatt, school-ma'am in *The Corn is Green*, and the old Cockney woman—she touches our lives. She spans the centuries.

One *in* a thousand—splendidly perceptive, human, she belongs to our century and its relationships. She is herself, Christian, dependable, beautiful. Helping with hand-luggage on our railway station, she looked up for a moment to shake me by the hand; in answer to my request for permission to quote her tribute to Lilian Baylis, she penned me a reply: 'Certainly, anyone who can make Lilian Baylis's work known has my blessing.'

My hope is that anyone able in the least degree to make her work known, shall have Heaven's blessing. Dame Sybil Thorndike, D.B.E., LL.D.

The people of the parish who provided her home and earliest setting, hardly knew what to make of things sometimes. Young Sybil and Russell loved to act; and were so high-spirited. A scarf, a home-made sword in scabbard, sheets, drapes from wherever they could be found, furnished their property-box. It was absorbing fun—and father, despite his bewildered parishioners, was the last to mind. He remembered that drama had its birth within the early Church. His young people understood what it was to be earnest—but not to be glum. Every hour as it came to them was too full of life for that!

When she must train for a vocation, Sybil set off for the Guildhall School of Music. Would she have made one of the world's great musicians? Nobody knows—nobody can know, brother Russell included. He kept an early photograph, taken when she was seventeen. When he came to set down her story, he was happy to find a place for it—and a caption: 'Sybil, arranged for her first pianoforte recital.' There was a second one, taken later—*then no more.* Had lively Sybil changed her mind? No! But something had happened that would have deeply disheartened many another and had changed it for her—trouble in her wrist, muscular cramp. It made it agony to span an octave. Only in the light of what came later—the wonderful, on-going gift to us—could brother Russell add, 'Never was an *apparent disaster* more fortunate.'

Musicianship impossible, she turned to the stage—natural enough, following youthful forays into the property-box. But this would be more than play—hard work. There was so much to be learned, apart altogether from her lines—and whoever learned more? Or carried through her offering to such a point of sensitivity and consummate art? At the end of years, the London *Observer* searched for words pregnant with warm appreciation, to say, 'Dame Sybil Thorndike has taken every kind of role from the saint to the harpy, from the she-demons of the Grand Guignol to the model wives and mothers of domestic comedy. She has always been able to combine the gritty sense of comedy with the emotional impact of tragedy.'

More than this, she has been able to combine a deeply religious experience with the demanding life of the theatre; an exacting need to travel, with the joys and responsibilities of wife, mother, home-maker, good citizen, neighbour, laughter-making friend, helper in progressive causes. All, a splendid whole! A glorious achievement! And not to be understood without the long-time theatre and family *rapport* with her distinguished husband, Sir Lewis Casson.

MY PRAYER

O God of creation, I rejoice in the inventiveness of youth;

in the riches of drama, and music;
in the loveliness of the human voice.
I rejoice in the words of the prophets;
in the poetry of the psalmists;
in modern statements of living truth.
I rejoice in men and women in our world
to whom goodness matters most;
from whose daily offering inspiration falls.
Let some of these great qualities of life find a place
in my own personality, I pray;
adding worth and beauty to all I am, and all I do.
In the name of Christ, our common Lord. AMEN

OUR PRAYER TOGETHER

O God, there is no good and lovely thing, but comes from you—
the laws of nature and the longings of our own hearts proclaim you!
From the beginning of time, men and women have hushed their hearts in your presence;
they have built their altars, and worshipped—and gone about their tasks in the world.
With the gifts you have lent to them, they have told great stories, and recited poems;
They have fashioned themselves homes, and supported each other in family and community life.
Quicken in us today, a new thankfulness for lovely and useful shapes, and colours, and textures;
for the fashionless qualities of human goodness, human joy, human dignity.
Give us pride in others' knowledge, others' accomplishments, others' service;
that in everyday give-and-take, we may know enrichment of living—to your greater glory. AMEN

PRINCE OF RAG-PICKERS

A little boy here, and another there, the world round, envisions himself a train-driver, a jockey, a sea-captain —but no one, in his wildest dreams, thinks of himself as a *rag-picker for Christ*. Nor did Pierre. His more mature wish was to be a missionary in Africa—but his health was never robust enough for that cruel climate. Instead, he found his way to Grenoble—in the high, airy, French Alps. And none of the hunted Jewish men and women doubted for a moment that God had guided him to the right place, as he risked all he had to bring them into the safety of Switzerland.

When at length—the war at an end—he became a member of the French parliament, he still seemed to be in the right place. He got possession of an old house in an unfashionable part of Paris. Its roof leaked, glass was out of some of its windows, it had no electric lights. Clearly, it needed a great deal of renovation; and each night—free of his daily responsibilities—Pierre came home, put on overalls, and got to work.

In time, he was joined by an ex-convict with nowhere to reckon on a roof, by a Czech refugee in the same plight, and by an ex-boxer—among a handful of others as hard-pressed. Pierre was the only one of them with any money in his pocket, and he shared what he had to meet their common need, calling this unusual community, 'The Companions of Emmaus'. Always in his mind was the post-resurrection experience of the two disheartened men walking to Emmaus—joined presently by Another (Luke 24). Just as they invited him in to the simple meal beneath their roof—and found, to their amazement, that he was none other than the living Christ—Pierre lived on the hope that his modern-day companions, dispirited, would find at his own table a like reality.

Near their old house—for more room when more men came—they set up a disused army-hut. Housing was so desperately hard to get. News reached him of one family with children, living under a piece of shabby canvas stretched against a hedge—this had spelled out death for two of the little ones. The Companions, led by Pierre—the Abbé Pierre, by this time—set themselves to do what they could to help the needy about them, even as they had been helped. From an assortment of old planks, they built a little hut; and the 'hedge family' moved in. But that was not all; soon others came on weary feet, hungry and unhappy, or hitch-hiking long distances—all placing their hope in the kind heart of 'the Abbé who helped the poor'.

It was not simple, now that Abbé Pierre had cut himself off from his earnings as a respected citizen. The Companions agreed there was no living without some money; so they set off in twos, through the back ways of the city, to gather scrap—to sort and sell to dealers what they could find. They found old clocks, and patiently repaired them; they dragged through the streets broken bicycles and prams. And above all things, they became *rag-pickers for Christ*.

The uncommonly harsh winter of 1954 put them severely to the test. But they did not fail. The authorities, respecting their humble effort, gave Abbé Pierre five precious minutes' broadcasting time. But what could he do, so briefly? From the many human stories of need known to him, he selected carefully, and drew a few word-pictures. And to this day, no one who chanced to hear them has forgotten. For many, a new experience of Christ-like compassion began with the words they heard: *'These are all your brothers!'*

MY PRAYER
O God, it is wonderful to receive your gift of daily

breath, along with your gift of daily bread;

It is wonderful to live in a pleasant place, with those whom I know, and love;

I would not forget those for whom the setting of life offers so little that is clean and comfortable;

So little that is a stimulus to work, and play—and a sense of satisfaction and pride in achievement.

Grant to mayors and councillors, and all responsible citizens, a patient wisdom;

Grant to ministers of the gospel of Christ, and to social workers, love translated in common concern.

Deliver from despair those who, having made a new start, fail once more;

Surround the discouraged with faithful friends, O God with perseverance, and the joy of triumph in the end. AMEN

OUR PRAYER TOGETHER

O God, you have sent us to school in this life we share—
　　with lessons that test all that we are;
　　with teachers of gathered experience;
You have given us the companionship of others—
　　so that we are never alone;
　　so that we add our little to the common experience.
We recall with joy the rich discoveries we have made—
　　the beauty of the earth, and sky;
　　and the daily lives of good people.
Only when we recall promptings disobeyed, duties unperformed,
　　are we truly humbled;
　　dependent on your forgiveness.
No earthly power can strengthen us wholly—no human love
　　satisfy us wholly.
　　Gracious God, hold us in our going out, and our coming in. Now, and ever. AMEN

A PRESENT-DAY POLICEWOMAN

'How did it all start for you?' I asked Liverpool police-woman Chief Superintendent Ivy Wood. My query was not concerned with women's work in general—I had read a good deal about that. Much water had run under the bridge since women first had a front place in many of the services—in Medicine, the Law, the Church. 'My entry', said Superintendent Wood, 'was in no way dramatic. Everyone, on the declaration of war, was joining up in one of the fighting forces. Family obligations stood in my way, but I jokingly said that if ever Manchester advertised for policewomen, I'd join. They did; and so started my police career!'

It is now over thirty-one years since this plump, pleasant officer, with an air of competence, put on uni-form. Some of England's cities had policewomen in the thirties, but Manchester lagged—as did Liverpool, to which Miss Wood, as sergeant, transferred to become inspector in charge of women newly recruited. Today, she is responsible for the 186 women in Liverpool's city force.

In sight of retirement though she is, the 'action' still goes on. 'There were days,' she reminded me, 'when a policewoman was a novelty. One was then expected "to pound the beat", and assume responsibility only for women and girls. It is encouraging to see how extensively women are employed in the force today. Though I still think', she added, 'that the basis of police work is going round on two feet. You meet and get to know people that way.'

Many young women coming forward as cadets today are much better educated than in the early days, with every prospect of employment eventually in some part of the dramatically widening range of activities. And

the times call for what they can bring. 'But important
still', added Miss Wood, 'is the ability to mix well with
people, without becoming too emotionally involved.'

From being early a helper in the Sunday school of
her church, she continues an eager interest in youth,
through membership of the Liverpool District Christian
Citizenship Committe; and vice-chairmanship of the
city's area in the Duke of Edinburgh's Award Scheme.
She is also a member of the city's Business and Professional Women's Club and of the Diocesan Board of
Moral Welfare, etc. People to Miss Wood are people
—though life is very different in many ways today.
Occasionally still, she confesses—though the officer has
small faith in it herself—a mother will bring an errant
daughter to her for 'a good talking to'.

In answer to my interest in unusual incidents, she
told of an early one, when three small filthy children
appeared, saying they were 'lost'. After taking down
their ages, and what details they could supply, she found
herself—with no one else at the office just then—wondering how she would keep them from fear. She remembered that the office held three wash-basins, so, to amuse
them, she set them to have a wash. Clearly, they had no
such luxuriant supply of hot water at home and, filling
up each of the basins to the brim, were soon having a
glorious time. Mother came at last, and carried them
off. 'But two days later,' said Miss Wood, 'two of them
appeared again, on the plea that they were "lost". They
had found a new interest in their lives!'

Personal relations with the police, she had to admit,
had deteriorated in some places—sex offences, shop-
lifting, and breaches of probation were in measure responsible for this. 'Many young offenders', she added,
'seem to lack all sense of guilt, and are greatly put out
at "being booked".' More distressing still, in certain
city areas, is a third generation of offenders. Always,
nowadays, there is also the traffic problem; the broken
home; the teen-ager off on a fling. Day and night, this

great service continues—advising, seeking, saving, inter-
preting the Law with justice and with mercy!

MY PRAYER

As the city I know best throbs on, O Lord, bless all
who live to help its common life—guardians of the Law,
social-workers, ministers, firemen, caretakers, cleaners.

All day long, and through the night, all your men and
women and young people have their needs met by
doctors, taxi-drivers, milkmen, artists, entertainers.

And there are the lonely, the foolish, the vicious, the
purposeless, the weak, the homeless.

Save me from pride if I am not of their company—
because I have needs, too. Law-abiding, home-loving,
church-going, I need much.

By your mercy, keep me; help me to obey your great
command to love my neighbour as I love myself.

But help me to love you best of all. And let my goodness today be gracious. AMEN

AMEN

OUR PRAYER TOGETHER

O God, strengthen us to live well and happily—to face
responsibility, and to mix well with our fellows.

We are thankful that you have not made us to
journey through life alone.

We are thankful for all that shared talk and experiences mean to us.

We are thankful for the many who have honoured us
with their friendship—and for the many with interests
like our own.

Enable us to be approachable, generous with time,
constructive and kind, in criticism.

And let us not save our best behaviour for strangers,
but be as considerate to those with whom we live.

We give thanks for them—for the plans we make,
the fun we share, and the joys we know together.

Bless all who cross our doorstep. AMEN

A MIGHTY ATOM

Father Kim's family had outgrown his purse by the time little Helen, the last but one, was born. There were eight children in the family. In Korea then, daughters were not always named—they were not counted important enough for that. In childhood, they were simply daughters of their fathers, later, wives of their husbands, and throughout the remainder of their lives, mothers of their sons. But the Kim family—poor in material things—was rich in affection. They named their new-comer—little imagining that today hers would be a name known the world round, and honoured as no other in her own country.

Always tiny—under five feet when fully adult, able to wear size three shoes—Helen was to rise to one of the greatest tasks of any woman in any country, as President of Ewha Women's University—*largest of its kind in the world*, with an enrolment of over eight thousand students!

When death caught up with her in 1970, those who knew her as president, as friend, as leader, had received much from her rich life. They marvelled as they reflected on how humbly she had begun her own education.

At that time, her two older sisters were already boarders at Korea's first school for girls. But little sister had to walk to and fro each day. And family finances were soon so low that the sisters who had advanced some distance in learning, had to return home. Anxious about Helen, her mother took her problem to the principal of the school. Miss Frey called her small pupil to her office after school, along with several others. All were shy. They had never spoken to their principal—they had seen her only far off as she led chapel sessions. It was not the thing, they were taught, to come near elders and superiors without being summoned, and they held Miss Frey in respect amounting almost to awe. Trembling, when her turn came, each child answered the questions put to her. Nodding and smiling, the principal then dismissed them.

Next day came the news that little Helen had been accepted as a scholarship pupil. It was a great relief to her anxious mother, at the heart of family struggles; and she straightway packed up for her the things she would need—bedding, towels, wash-basin, rice bowl with spoon and chop-sticks, and a chest for her few clothes.

Those who played and worked with Helen knew well, from the start, her eagerness to learn. Some girls, it was understood, had to 'steal' their education by hiding behind screens where their brothers were instructed by hired teachers.

In time, Helen graduated from Ewha College; later, from Ohio Wesleyan University with a B.A. degree; then from Boston University Graduate School with an M.A.; and lastly, from Teachers' College of Columbia University with a Ph.D.—the *first woman from Korea* to earn that coveted honour. All this and more she achieved over the years—despite a spell when she was smitten down with tuberculosis; a time when she companied with fear and danger during her country's struggle for independence, when many of her close friends were in prison; a time when she was summoned to serve as Director of Public Information during the grim Korean War; and when, bombs falling on her college, she had to flee with students and staff, and set up in exile, making do with tents and hastily erected shacks.

During all these strenuous undertakings, Dr Helen Kim represented her Church, and the Y.W.C.A. at boards and conferences, travelling far; and her country at the United Nations, in New York. So she conferred, wrote, administered, prayed—and, returning after a stressful interval, to find her beloved college in ruins, set-to, and built again.

And this is one place 'where the action is' today!

MY PRAYER

O God, I remember too lightly my early schooling—following

> my first lessons at home;
> my play-times, and working hours;
> all wonderful gifts from you.

I thank you for my expanding interests of maturity;

> for truths and treasurable things shared;
> for splendid companions, for challenges;
> for opportunity spelling out satisfaction.

Keep me always true to the best I know, and am—

> when the rights of others are wantonly by-passed;
> when irresponsible standards are condoned;
> when selfishness is enthroned as of first importance.

Enthrone in my heart today all that is lovely and of good report, all that fosters true enquiry, and supports honest learning.

When things go ill with me, deliver me from self-pity; when things go well, from complacency and pride. In the name of Christ. AMEN

OUR PRAYER TOGETHER

O God, let no short-sightedness of ours stand in the way of your will being done today:

We pray for teachers and lecturers; for members of school committees and college boards—

> for modest homes where funds are short and books few;
> for young people who must earn to meet costs;

We pray for those, on the other hand, who take all, as of easy right—

> the brilliantly endowed but irresponsible;

the wasters of powers on drink or drugs.

O God, strengthen the vital friendship of all who offer help to the discouraged, the misfits, the rebels. And bless our on-going adventure. AMEN

ACTION IN QUETTA

The blue envelope lay uppermost on my morning's mail. I recognized the handwriting. Immediately Dr Henry Holland's background flashed through my mind; then I slashed open the envelope to learn what new thing he had to tell me.

His parents' passing thought that he might be a parson seemed now a long way back; even his own dream, while at Edinburgh University doing medicine, that he might land a pleasant country practice near a trout stream.

By striking contrast, he had been appointed to Quetta. At first, he had been forced to ask, 'Where's that?' But he was soon to find out—fitted up with his medical kit, sun topee, dark glasses, spine pad and cholera belt. It awaited him—away beyond Karachi—on the infamous North-West Frontier!

Blood feuds and banditry were commonplace in Quetta. Fanatical Muslims counted the murder of an 'infidel' a meritorious act, and the swords of many were stained with the blood of missionaries and Afghan converts. One—Abdul Karim, son of a Muslim judge in Quetta—had actually been taken in chains to a distant place, and beaten. But he had refused to deny his new-found Christian faith; whereupon his captors had cut off first one arm, then the other. Next, they beheaded him.

From the outset, young Dr Henry's service had been among such people—very far from his university dream! In time, he had got to know his hospital staff, to respect them, and to develop his surgery. Soon he was helping to restore sight to blind eyes. And this was to become his outstanding contribution through the years. News of 'the man who opens the eyes of the blind' travelled fast, and far, through that cruelly hot, searing Frontier. And the time came when patients were threading their way to him through the passes from as far away as the city of Shikarpur, a good two hundred miles of rugged travel. The preaching of Christianity had been forbidden in this stronghold of Hinduism. Dr Henry made a journey up-country for three weeks to spy out how things were, and whilst there, in that brief time, managed to operate on four hundred patients. Greatly impressed, the banker in the city, who had himself sent patients, begged the missionary doctor to make an annual visit.

Astutely, Dr Henry agreed to return—but on two conditions: one, that a hospital must be provided, and all expenses of the treatment met; the other, that the Doctor and his staff must be granted a free right to preach. The Christian faith was, after all, the mainspring of all they did. The city leaders protested; but in the end had to submit. 'I'll bet', Dr Henry liked to boast, with a chuckle, 'Shikarpur is the first city to be opened to Christianity at the point of a cataract-knife!'

The hospital ready, the team were soon performing as many as twelve hundred cataract operations, and two thousand other operations of various kinds, during their six-week clinic.

All this I recalled; also, how Dr Henry—Sir Henry Holland—had been offered high posts at fabulous pay, to go to America, and elsewhere. 'But you can't put a price-tag on a fellow's love for his people,' came always his simple reply; whilst, to his two young doctor sons and their staff, he kept saying, till he left Quetta: *'If we Christians cannot live and out-love any other religion, we do not deserve to win!'* And that's still the spirit there today, 'where the action is'!

MY PRAYER
O God, our Father, we recall that Jesus' concern for men and women rose out of his love for you;
    that he set out 'steadfastly to go up to Jerusalem',

fulfilling all the way his given task.

Give to those of us who bear his name today the same readiness to follow his lead;

Give us tenderness with others' limitations and hurts, so that through all our serving they may see our Lord.

We are not worthy of a place in such glorious company, but you can, in your mercy, make use of what we bring in love. AMEN

OUR PRAYER TOGETHER

O God, you have given us many talents, and have allowed us to serve you here in all manner of ways—

we are glad about this.

To some of us you have given artistic gifts; to others, the practical head and hand;

To some of us you have given a love of intimate detail; to others great sweeping purposes;

To some of us you have set a place of service in the home, with little children; and others, far away.

Give us courage to make our response instant, and whole-hearted, whatever the challenge you set.

Let no remembrance of past failure spoil our readiness to try again—trusting more deeply.

Open our eyes, that we may sense your nearness— using us, keeping us in joy and sorrow, bringing us with thankfulness at last to our eternal home. AMEN

CHEERS FOR ROGER!

Paraplegics have become as commonly known now to many of us as plums were once, in a childhood orchard.

But young Roger Arnett's struggles started before he knew much of either. His parents were hard-pressed to provide for their family—added to that, there was health to contend with. Mother fell ill with pneumonia; father lacked the diet he needed for such hard work as he did; and young Roger fell through the trap-door into the cellar.

Arriving at Corunna, a few miles from the biggest town the junior members of the family had so far seen —with all that they owned on their backs—they began again. It was not simple—roads and fields were just then flooded, and furniture and clothing had somehow to be bought.

At his new school, Roger felt shy in his made-over suit, and in his shoes re-soled with thick cardboard. It was good when father had his day off, and together as a family they could walk in the country roundabout. Such recreation cost nothing, and they enjoyed mother's uncanny knowledge of the countryside—of trees and herbs and flowers—and, on occasion, there were nuts to gather.

By the time Roger had reached twelve, Irving eleven, and Vivian eight, they had managed to acquire second-hand bicycles—that meant they could go further. But it was *on his own two feet* that Roger was to come to fame. He longed to become an athlete—and in time managed to do so. And a very outstanding one at that! His name was passed from mouth to mouth with pride.

Till there came a day in 1931, when the car in which he was travelling to a distant sports-gathering, over-turned in a blinding snow storm. When Roger came to, it was plain that he was grievously hurt. Only later did specialists admit that he would be paralysed for life.

Very little was then known of paraplegia—to most only a hard name for a hard struggle. And Roger did struggle. There could never again, he told himself, be headlines in the sports-papers: 'Roger Arnett cross-country flash of State Normal team . . .' 'Arnett sets a new four-mile mark . . .' 'Arnett leads team-mates to third championship . . .' All finished!

But though he couldn't know it, a day would come when there would be headlines of another kind. Roger—handicapped—was making headway in a race against greater odds. Handicapped herself, by polio, his young wife supported him in every way. Together, they welcomed into their home three adopted children, and Roger and La Verna made it a happy home. Roger pushed himself around in a wheel-chair, swinging out of it—as he had need—into his car seat. Fortunately, his shoulders, arms and hands possessed great strength.

Strength of another kind that came to his aid, was his faith in God. And within and without the family home, his wife shared this. A time came when together they accepted still other new claims—Roger was set apart as a chaplain, that, in the special way he was so well qualified for, he might minister in homes and hospitals. Now, when—out of faith shared with the handicapped, along with games of chess, and talk, and laughter—his name appears in the headlines, it is as Vice-President of the American Federation of the Physically Handicapped!

MY PRAYER

O God, give me courage to meet well what life brings—
to face the unknown and the untried;
to make light of physical handicaps, in purposeful
living.
Bless all those who live under the same roof with me—

in every problem we face, save us from self-pity;
in any faltering relationship, let us know forgiveness and love.

Keep me continually courteous, and cheerful, especially
when I am overtired;
when I am tempted to take a short-cut, against
commonsense.

Keep me, strong in faith, in any situation that frightens
me;
if I must venture among complete strangers;
if I must spend time in hospital.

So bind together in splendid daily living, all tied to me
by
blood, and responsibility,
common suffering, and hope. In Christ's name.
                                                    AMEN

OUR PRAYER TOGETHER

We are endlessly grateful that you have 'set the solitary
in families';
the lonely and crippled amidst sympathy;
the enthusiastic before tasks crying to be done.

We are endlessly thankful that you have called us to
bear each others'
burdens, in the business of living, day by day;
and as patiently, special tests laid before us.

We are endlessly grateful that new knowledge of accident, and disease,
is being developed amongst us;
and that new occupations and interests are being
offered the handicapped.

We are endlessly grateful that the faith given us by our
Master, Christ,
is adequate in life's emergencies;
is a rich experience when life is full.

Forgive us for any lack of gratitude, that we so dislike
when we see it in others; any failure in cheerfulness, and
lack of consideration for those who serve us; any

hesitancy in sharing gladly with the sick, and the lonely, and the discouraged.

In your presence no darkness can overwhelm us; even death has not the last word! All praise and glory be yours! AMEN

THREE KNOCKS IN THE NIGHT

Famine comes often to India. But this one brought death to as many as three million people. It was unforgettable.

Little Ida Scudder—only six—helped her doctor father feed the starving. But by the time she had reached her teens, she had firmly made up her mind that she wanted to be neither a missionary nor a doctor. There were enough of both already in the Scudder family. She had other ideas. As long as she could remember, she had been familiar with the story of grandfather, who had turned his back on New York, to become the first American missionary-doctor in India. A thrilling but costly adventure! Dr John and his wife had lost by death a cherished two-year-old; and later, two tiny babes as well. In time, they had also to spare their growing sons, one by one, to be schooled away from them—Henry, William, Joseph, Ezekiel, Jared, Silas and John—all seven! And it got no easier. (It was John who eventually became Ida's father.)

But Ida stuck to her plan as the years marched on for her. Then, one night—when she had returned home from her own school in America—something unexpected happened. She was sitting alone in her room on the ground floor, just off the verandah. And presently she heard hurried steps, and a knock. Who could it be? Even whilst she wondered, a distressed voice called, 'Amah, amah! I have come to you in great trouble!' It was a young Brahmin who stood before Ida. His wife was about to have a baby. Hearing that the daughter of the doctor had returned from America, he sought her, distraught, to come and help his wife. But all that she could reply was that she knew nothing of such matters—

it was her father who was the doctor. 'But it is against our custom,' was all the young man could answer—he was unable to let a man attend his wife. And he disappeared into the night.

Again Ida was disturbed. Her immediate thought was that it was the young Brahmin husband back to say that he had changed his mind. But no—it was another, a Mohammedan, with a like request. And to him Ida had, perforce, to give the same disappointing answer.

'Evidently,' years older, years later she found herself commenting on that night, 'God knew I was not sufficiently conscience-stricken, because yet another appeared from the darkness, with the same appeal.' He was a high-caste Hindu. It was a night never to be forgotten —and it changed her life. Despite her firm stand, she knew then that she had to become a doctor. And, for those 'three knocks in the night', an innumerable company this day thanks God.

Graduating, in time, from Cornell, Ida came back to India, to involve herself in its superstitions, its ignorance, its desperate need. Her first little hospital was no larger than ten feet by twelve—but in two years, five thousand out-patients had been treated there. And Dr Ida laid plans for greater things—to train young Indian women themselves as doctors. 'You might get three willing,' said the authorities. 'If you get six, you have the Government's permission to start.' A hundred and fifty-one came forward, to everyone's amazement; and Dr Ida picked eighteen! It was a start! Being herself one of our day's outstanding gynaecologists, she battered tirelessly for her beloved Vellore School of Nursing, from 1909 on; and for Vellore Medical Missionary School for Women, founded in 1918 and later up-graded to a Medical College. And the very name 'Vellore' was to become famous the world round—before smiling, silver-haired Dr Ida's death. A triumph! Now, years later, in 1970, only thirty-five of Vellore's total staff of 2,616 are from abroad, with all but a few departments headed by Indian personnel, most of them its own Christian graduates.

MY PRAYER

O God, I am glad that in this age of guided missiles, men and women can be guided, too. I bless you for those through whom you have worked wonders, and pushed forward programmes of health.

In this day, when scores of vocations are open to young people on the theshold of service, let none of us fail in tender concern.

Lighten our journey upon this human way; let what help we can give, be as wholly and instantly given as that of many known to us since the traveller on the Jerusalem-Jericho road.

I ask this in the name of my Lord, who first told of the Good Samaritan to his humble listeners, and questioner. I would be one of his listeners now—here with ready hands, and caring heart.

Let there be nothing in today's opportunities of which I shall be sorry when the sun is set, or when at the end of life's day, I come at last to my eternal home. AMEN

OUR PRAYER TOGETHER

O God, our Father, you have entrusted to us powers of body and mind, not least the lively gift of imagination, by which we enter into others' troubles. Quicken us afresh just now as we pause in this place of renewal.

Bless all who—like Dr Ida Scudder—battle against odds, to bring healing and laughter into human lives. Give patience and encouragement to all who serve in drab places.

Quicken in us all—within our setting of privilege—concern for the 'masses'—not 'masses' to you, but men and women and little children, everlasting spirits.

We pray for all who lack the decencies of life—who

lie down in squalor, and waken in squalor; who lie down
in hunger, and waken in hunger; who lie down in hopelessness, and waken the same.

We pray especially for all who as yet have no one to
turn to. Hear their cry, and raise them helpers, O Lord
of wholeness. A M E N

A GALLANT TRIO

Nancy Polkinghorne's red telephone is not the only bright spot in her room—far from it—though she would be completely lost without it. It is her link with the great outside world, her 'medium of involvement', for those who choose high-sounding terms, though she would never speak of it that way. A polio victim, for years now she has been confined to her room. But she loves people —and there is hardly a busier person anywhere. A one-time typist and book-keeper, 'I now print my letters like this,' she wrote me in a recent letter, 'with my left hand, and sign my name with my right.' She lives in Adelaide—a large-hearted citizen, a loyal, though absentee Methodist. 'An odd person, you might say,' were her words to me, with that gentle humour she exercises as one of God's good gifts. Added to it is enormous courage and hope.

We are not strangers. During ten years of Church-youth leadership, a number of my books came her way —beginning with *Through Open Windows*. It doesn't surprise me, in the light of subsequent events, that she sets that book of mine—with its appealing title—first among her favourites. For even more important than windows in her room are 'windows' in her mind and spirit.

When suddenly illness struck, Len Polkinghorne was bank-manager in a little Australian town among the rolling hills. With Nancy rushed into hospital, he and their two young sons, ten and fifteen, were left to manage as best they could. Little was known of polio in 1949 and, for fear, of contagion, nobody, at first, came near. Between 9 a.m. and 6 p.m. for weeks—even when work and school called—little Ken remained in quarantine. His pent-up loneliness showed up later, when, on Mother's Day 1953, Nancy came back—unloaded and wheeled into her home—to face on the back door a poster with the one word, 'HOME!' In the passage were coloured streamers and another poster, 'WELCOME HOME', and on her bedroom door, 'AND BLOOMIN' WELL STAY THIS TIME'. With a partly trained nurse, house-keeper, family, neighbours and a physiotherapist, they tackled a new start. It was not easy.

There was that day when Ken, at fourteen, was sent home from school in pain—specialists operated, and re-moved a lump in his groin. The dread report said he had cancer of the lymph glands; and would be unlikely to live more than two years. With thankfulness, Nancy re-lates—now that two years have made way for twelve—that 'he is very much alive, a high-school teacher, with his loved wife.'

'The Bank moved us back to Adelaide, in time—handy to Wesley College, where Max was training for the ministry. We made another start. Somebody,' says Nancy, 'suggested we buy a duplicating-machine, and a typewriter. Another made me a sloping tray to place across my wheel-bed. To our joy, Max married his school-time friend Margaret; the world seemed a good place. Then out at his work—with his B.A., L. Th. and Dip. R.E.—Max was suddenly killed in a road accident, Margaret and their little family, left.'

And Nancy herself? Unable to use her fingers as formerly, she has, for years now, operated her bright red telephone for a hospital Bed Service on behalf of the Geriatric and Custodial Hospital of South Australia. 'A mouthful!' she admits. But altogether she has over forty hospitals and rest-homes on her list; and day-in, day-out, spends time patiently listening, in the hope of matching revealed needs to available facilities. 'People in trouble need a listener,' she says, 'even when we can't help immediately. And it even helps, at times, to know that I'm in this position.'

Nancy also works, through her red phone, for Adelaide's Kitchen, 'Meals on Wheels'—with rosters of drivers. Added to this, she and Len involve themselves in the Phoenix Society—its magazine, and programme designed to help handicapped folk help themselves. Of late, a sheltered workshop has been established, for over two hundred, with Len a home visiting convener.

A gallant trio! For that bright red telephone must be counted in!

MY PRAYER

O Lord of life, save me from ever taking my health for granted. It is a wonder that no single breath I draw is outside your knowledge, your love, your care.

If life, at this time, lays special burdens upon me, save me from self-pity, from despair. Quicken my faith, my resolute purpose. You have promised that those who wait upon you shall renew their strength; let me experience the reality of this.

To those living in narrow physical limits, widen I pray, the bounds of mind and spirit. This I ask in the name of Christ. AMEN

OUR PRAYER TOGETHER

Gracious God, as we move about the world today, let us not be so absorbed in our own affairs that we forget others at home—

We would remember especially all handicapped by illness; all who tend them; and all who devote their trained energies to the discovery of fresh, more effective treatments.

Without waiting for all our problems to be resolved, all our secret questions answered, we would do what we can to make life interesting for all such. Grant them a sense of your undergirding presence; give them patience, when time drags, when reports are long in coming.

Grant your blessing on all families who must cope with invalidism, with chronic ill-health, with accident

IN THE THEATRE

Young Peter Baillie—like most healthy youngsters born in Hastings, New Zealand—took the golden sun that bathed his limbs, and town, and orchard-lands, very much for granted. It was a blessing that he knew day after day. School took him to Palmerston North, and work to Wellington, the capital. And from place to place —first as a boy and then as a young man—Peter carried with him a gift of song. He sang in school and church choirs, and in the capital's Phoenix Choir he sang in many oratorios—the *Messiah*, *Elijah*, the *St Matthew Passion* and Benjamin Britten's *War Requiem*.

And from his home-country he moved to Australia, where he met Lois, soon to be his wife. Still more journeys called. With his precious gift, in 1966 Peter found himself singing in the Salzburg Festival. Everything was more mellow in that lovely old birth-place of Mozart—even its sun that fell on river, cathedral, castle and winding streets. Performances of Mozart's operas at Salzburg originated the summer music festivals which are now an annual event.

But still more journeys called. Peter Baillie has sung in many European capitals since; he has taken part in a Royal Command performance—being presented to Queen Elizabeth and the Duke of Edinburgh. Radio and television have carried his song to many in their homes.

His own home is now in Vienna—where he is a full-time singer in the city's *Volksoper* (people's opera), one of the two professional companies in the Austrian capital. *Volksoper* performs works—including many operettas—in the German language only.

In Vienna, the young tenor and his wife belong to the Vienna Community Church, a basically non-conformist Protestant Church. One of the two English-speaking churches in the city, it has a membership a little above two hundred and fifty—and, what makes it a rich fellowship, they come from thirteen different nations, representing some thirty branches of the Church in the world. Peter Baillie—a Presbyterian—is actively engaged as chairman of Christian education on the church board, along with members from Japan, the United States of America, and Canada.

He is frequently asked how his Christian witness, and work in the theatre affect one another. Peter, of course, is a man of spirit, as well as body and mind.

'In the theatre,' he admits, 'one is exposed to more opportunity to be non-Christian than perhaps a person in more normal occupations. One is involved in a communication medium where there is a certain amount of glamour. The temptation is to use this for selfish ends. Working in the theatre, one is rather divorced from ordinary society—and people who want to break away have a chance to do so.'

Asked about the effect emotionally of the characters he must play continually, Peter Baillie, the Christian, admits the difficulties. 'If you are playing the big hero type of character, you are in danger of transferring this attitude to your own character, and also of taking advantage of adulation.

'Then,' he adds, 'there is the aspect of the words that are sung—much more penetrating than the communication of, say, playing a musical instrument. And there are the visual parts of opera, lighting, costumes and make-up. Of course, one of the difficulties that a Christian singer comes up against is how to put Christianity into a character he may be playing who is foul and obscene. Take Faust, for instance; he is a man who sells his soul for physical pleasure and worldly gain—an age-old theme—and who brings sorrow and distress, ruin, madness and death to the girl, Marguerite. Such a man could not be further from my idea of life. But if one bears in mind that the character being played is in fact the personification of a universal problem, the opera does have something to say to us now.'

For Peter Baillie, the setting of daily living—home, theatre, as well as Church is 'where the action is'. '*If one has a Christian faith*,' he sums up, '*this should show in everything!*'

MY PRAYER

O Lord of life, save me from the subtle temptations inherent in my daily work;

Grant that my tongue, which so easily sings your praise, may always speak your truth;

Grant that my feet, which have walked to your house of worship, may walk as surely among men and women in the workaday world;

Grant me strength to bear a good witness—to serve here and now the everlasting interests of your Kingdom of holy love.

In the name of Christ. AMEN

OUR PRAYER TOGETHER

O God, you have called us into a partnership of infinite variety—you have given us many gifts.

You have chosen to create this world in which you have set us, with room for all kinds of service.

You have given us wonderful differences of race, and colour, and outlook, that we might all be enriched.

To some of us you have granted the gift of song, to others the meaningful silence.

Some of us you have led about the wide world—others of us you have set in familiar ways, to witness at home.

Keep us faithful to you, wherever this day finds us—responsive, sincere, and joyous, doing what we can, to the best of our ability.

To your honour and glory. AMEN

DOWN-TO-EARTH RELIGION

Gifford Towle had reason to throw over the old proverb, 'Neither a borrower nor a lender be'.

When the rains failed, the cattle began to waste to skeletons, and die. He was in India to direct a demonstration farm for the Church of Christ, U.S.A. The skies above his head offered nothing but a merciless glare, and every vestige of green in Vadala dried up.

Two years before, a well had been dug—a very deep well—but now the problem was to get *enough* water up, and *fast enough*.

In the emergency, news of the invention of a new type of diesel pump reached him. But there was no one to answer all his questions—no one had seen it. There was nothing that could satisfy his need, short of a hurried journey over the two hundred hot miles to Bombay. There, he examined every point adding up to promise, of one of the first off the production line. And he bought it—though it cost five hundred dollars!

Back in Vadala—his money spent—he tossed out the old proverb, and borrowed a thousand feet of piping. And in a short time, he was on the way to performing miracles. His new pump—thanks to the piece of borrowed piping—was soon lifting the life-giving water up out of that deep well.

News got around, and worried farmers from far and near came to see with their own eyes what they had all but rejected as rumour. Water out of the earth! Green feed for the animals coming up out of the thirsty earth!

'Lend us your pump,' they begged of Gifford Towle, 'so that we can do the same.' But he had to refuse to completely part with that old proverb; if he lent out his pump, what miracle he had already performed would be instantly cut short. Then life would cease.

Instead, he managed to get his Church to buy a second pump—to hire out to the worried villagers. The fee was small, and the first man to apply for the pump was Madhu Rao Mali. He desperately wanted a 'green miracle' for his animals, too. But he was so poor, he had to begin still further back, with the plea, 'Lend me the money, to hire the pump—and I'll pay you back next harvest'. But it could not be; or where would the undertaking end? But the village money-lender was ready to negotiate, at twenty-five per cent.

The following season, Madhu Rao Mali came to Gifford Towle with a new plan: 'Buy me a pump of my own!'

'But how can you afford five hundred dollars for a pump,' he had to ask, 'when you could not find money to hire one for a week?' But the Indian farmer was insistent; and soon the secret was out.

Madhu Rao Mali's family was a large one—uncles, cousins, wives, sons. And the 'green miracle' that no one alone could possibly achieve, became a reality. One sold a bullock, another a goat, a third a piece of treasured jewellery. And, in the sale of the various possessions, the whole sum was found.

The protest of fellow-villagers, 'You've gone crazy,' fell on deaf ears. And it wasn't long before they could boast some of the best crops to be seen anywhere. Gifford Towle's Christian enterprise, and the village family's energy have brought a new day. Within ten years, four hundred and seventy diesel pumps are bringing to the surface new life around Vadala.

MY PRAYER
Gracious Father, I would not let the comfort of my situation lull me into forgetfulness of others—
  in excessively hot lands;
  in overcrowded lands;
  in poor lands.

Stimulate all inventors and technicians who give us new tools, to bring water to the thirsty earth; to relieve the burdens of the hard-pressed, beyond their strength; to produce food enough for family needs, for beasts, and market.

Bless all modern missionaries who help in terms of mechanical direction; all who share in the stewardship of the earth; all who, through such ventures, translate through exhausting, sweaty days, Christian caring.

Quicken in the hearts of the dispirited who receive much, the sincere desire to give much.

Prosper the prayers, O Lord, and the giving of those of us afar, set on extending the Bible-days' feeding of 'the five thousand'.

Whilst 'man does not live by bread alone'—without bread, rice, fish, the equivalent, he cannot live at all.

You have made us all—wherever we live—body, mind and spirit. And in each we need to be nourished constantly.

Deliver from wastefulness those of us favoured in our birthplace—and quicken responsibility in our farmers, merchants, distributors.

Save us from greedily wanting more, while some have so little—our brothers and sisters on the earth.

Our Father, hear us in these prayers. AMEN

OUR PRAYER TOGETHER

For each returning day, we give thanks, O God—
> for its beauty, its work, its human needs met;
> for the delight of human relationships;
> for leisure at day's end, and laughter to lighten all we share.

We thank you, above all, for your Church in the world—and in the setting where we know it best; for the redeeming, renewing gospel of Christ.

We thank you for every testing experience that has helped us grow in our Christian faith and service—despite our stupidities. AMEN

THEY ARE ALL PEOPLE

The ugly modern term 'geriatric' repels most of us; but not Edith James. To her it stands for people—needy people, loved people. And that makes all the difference to the Supervising Matron of the Presbyterian Social Service Association of Otago, New Zealand.

I asked her lately how it came about that in the youthful fullness of her powers, she started nursing elderly people? I knew it wasn't for lack of qualifications—or experience; nor was it for want of a job; nor age. I hardly needed to put my question about the special skills she possesses—though I did put it. 'It does mean dedication, of course,' said she. 'Shift work—for ours is a twenty-four-hour-a-day service, seven days of the week —calls for that. But there's an indefinable "something" about this type of nursing. Patience? Yes, of course— and an ear to hear what needs to be heard, and the wisdom to recognize what doesn't need to be heard; a smile in sad situations, sympathy without sentimentality. But I guess', she added, 'it's basically a good, real love of God, and one's fellow-men.' Beyond that, there didn't seem much to ask. But Edith James added: 'I am one of those fortunate people who has always been loved, and known security; so it isn't hard for me to love. I am happy in a chat, and I can listen. Laughs?' she continued, at my next question, 'there have been loads. Over one hated bath, an old gentleman flung his words at me: "All my life it has been women—my mother, then my wife, daughters—and now *you!*" *But he had his bath!*' she added.

Off-duty, Miss James—loving young people, as she loves old—is interested in Girl Guides, the Girls' Brigade, women's groups. Registered Nurses' Association meetings, reading, drama, and handcrafts; which means that loving God, loving people, *she is alive*!

To fill out the background for me, she ran over a succession of events—for nothing happens all at once. After working in an office, she took a nurse's training. Then followed first sister's work at a sanatorium; a health camp; Plunket District work among mothers and babies; Green Lane Hospital, T.B. section; service as a field officer with the Child Welfare Department; midwifery; ten years' tropical life as a nurse in New Guinea with the Methodist Mission; and finally four years back in New Zealand as matron of a Methodist Eventide Home.

'Seeds are sown early,' she suggested. 'A holiday job in Sydney perhaps planted mine. But it slept until I returned from New Guinea, when I vividly recalled seeing a notice erected in a grass paddock outside Hamilton—set to catch passers-by. "On this site", it said, "is to be built 'Tamahere Eventide Home' . . ." Had it actually been built? I had no idea. But I sought out an answer; and applied for a position, and got it.

'There are so many old people in our community these days—and nursing among them is a challenge to me.' After a pause, she added, '*They are all people.* In their frailty, they trust us, and we give them security. I chose to be a *geriatric* nurse—to answer your pointed question—because of the satisfaction in using basic nursing skills for long-term caring. Of people are built up warm, deep, loving, satisfying relationships. Many of these people have actually lived exciting lives, and still retain fine qualities of personality.'

MY PRAYER
O God, I give thanks that all life is your gift—morning, midday, and evening.

I seek your special blessing just now, on all who begin to feel life's evening drawn out;

Diminished strength spells limitations—of sight, hearing, and physical enterprise.

Many long-time friends have already gone upon their

way—memories of them, still precious;

Sweeter than honey, more treasurable than gold, are the associations with good people—and good living.

Many small worries that at the time seemed great, have long since sunk into perspective;

Many tasks that in mere human strength would have proved overwhelming, have been accomplished—and laid as offerings at your feet.

Again and again, when we seemed no longer able to hold on to you, you have held on to us;

And now, till I come in sight of my journey's end, I would offer thanks for all your goodness—joy for joy, love for love.

In the name of Jesus Christ, our Lord. A M E N

OUR PRAYER TOGETHER
O God, we give thanks for the total experience of human life—

> for tradesmen, technicians, and artists of true intent;
> for painters and poets, for singers and story-tellers;
> for teachers, and all through whom you have given a rich heritage of beauty, truth and goodness.

We give thanks for dreamers of fair cities, of spinning wheels, humming machines, and people's needs met.

We give thanks for all work of honest and exact precision—for all courageous enough to drop outmoded ideas.

We give thanks for all who have considered people above profits and material things.

Let the skills of our hands bless you this day—in the name of the Carpenter of Nazareth, who served so well.

A M E N

A NEW MAN, A NEW NAME

The young Hindu proudly arched his first three fingers, and scooping up a ball of curry and rice, in the Indian fashion, popped it into his mouth. Millions did it every day without a thought, but there was something very special about it when Krishnamurthy did it. It was a moment never to be forgotten, when Dr Paul came within hearing and heard his patient's exclamation.

Dr Paul Brand, serving at the Christian Medical Centre in Vellore, South India, had not forgotten going to visit a leprosy sanatorium. It was a less sombre place than he had expected. The patients grew their own food, wove their own bandages, and gave each other injections. But it was all done against great difficulties—disfigured faces, blind eyes, and stumps of fingers and toes.

It was their hands that the doctor noticed most— hands folded in the Indian manner of greeting, hands outstretched in the Western style of hand-shake, hands clutching dishes. Stiffly set, unable to flex fingers, they were more like claws of birds or animals than human hands. He couldn't get the sight of them out of his mind. Leprosy, he knew, was being cured in India by the new drugs, as in many other parts of the world. He knew also that the disease was now known to be less infectious than was at one time feared. But these awful hands, he said to himself, why wasn't somebody doing something about them?

And it was not long before Dr Paul Brand realized that this was a challenge that he must himself accept. It was, of course, a mighty challenge—there were at least ten to fifteen million sufferers in the world, including those he had seen. Not all were as fortunate; not all had received their measure of attention. But they still looked a pitiful lot, with those poor hands.

Soon he began singling out one whose hands could hardly be made worse, on whom he could experiment. And Krishnamurthy was that one—and was willing. In reply to the doctor's questioning, he shrugged his shoulders, as if to say, 'Do what you will. I might as well be dead as like this.' And it was true—he had ulcers on the soles of his feet, and miserable, claw-like hands utterly useless. What good was his education, and the fact that he could speak several languages? His good position gone, all he could do now was sit and beg.

After many months of preparation, of careful testing and surgery, news got out that a leprosy claw was being changed into a hand again! And what was in every way as miraculous, a despondent beggar was becoming a man again! His eyes now were bright, his mind alert to what each day offered, he was even heard to laugh!

The foremost question puzzling Krishnamurthy was basic: Why was the doctor prepared to do all this for him? He was without any special claim—even his own family had turned him out. The answer, of course, when he discovered it, was that day-in, day-out, the doctor served as Master, one whom he called Jesus Christ. In time, his amazed patient asked for further instruction—and baptism; he wanted to become a Christian, too. And like many a one in New Testament times—and since—knowing himself a new man, the young Hindu asked for a new name. He chose the name 'John'—the one beloved. And as such, faces life today.

To teach new skills to new men, the New Life Centre has been founded, to the glory of Christ—just one more modern centre, where '*the action is*'!

MY PRAYER
O God, I am glad that you are a God of broken things mended,
  of lost things found;
  of perplexing questions answered gloriously;
  of devoted servants in all the earth!

While I give thanks for my faculties, gifts of heart and hand,

>   I do not forget others who know nothing of these—
>   of the joy of movement;
>   of the sweet satisfaction that simple achievements
>   hold.

I give you thanks for medical and nursing services available—

>   now reaching to places of desperate need;
>   to men and women in despair;
>   to many seeking deliverance from sin, fear and
>   insecurity, which cripple spirits as well as bodies.

I love to recall that no one who sought our Lord whilst he was here among men, the Great Physician, was ever made to feel a nuisance, was ever turned away unhelped. And this is the great miracle still. For this I praise you!

AMEN

OUR PRAYER TOGETHER

It is wonderful to be alive, O God, in this century of so many possibilities—

>   to join with others in work and play;
>   to share a measure of health and movement;
>   to come and go at will.

We are full of happiness that you have shown us your power in the framework of the world—

>   in the seasons that come and go;
>   in the calm beauty of moon and stars;
>   in the tides that ebb and flow.

But most of all, we marvel at the compassion of Christ, shown us in the Gospels —

>   in the forgiveness of our faults;
>   in the strengthening of our wills;
>   in the sustaining sense of his presence. Today, and
>   always. AMEN

CARAVANS AND BRIGANDS

Caravans are not part of our days and nights—much less brigands. No wonder the three gentle ladies held me enthralled.

One summer morning in 1923, after twenty years in Hwochow, they had set off—not just to visit a friend at the end of a few miles—to cross the *world's largest desert*! The famous Gobi—or infamous, as one chose to think of it—lay at the heart of Asia. The Chinese wrote its name in two ideographs or picture-letters, meaning 'Wall of Spears'.

But Mildred Cable, and Evangeline and Francesca French took a thoroughly realistic view of the undertaking. They had lived in China too long to venture foolishly, ill-prepared. There were hazards enough when all had been done. Countless others who had turned their backs on the ways of civilization, to go off into the desert, had never been heard of again.

At the agreed moment, these three cultured ladies had set off in a lumbering mule-cart with high wheels and a rough hooded roof.

It had actually taken them two years to reach the city of Kiayukwan—the 'Mouth of China', where the ancient country ended and the Gobi Desert began. By this time, they travelled in a new cart made entirely of wood without a piece of metal, even a nail. Its great wheels stood taller than any one of them—eight feet— capable, they believed, of carrying them through rivers, and across seas of mud if necessary. Its hood was thatched with dry grass. And they had exchanged their mule for a strong, sturdy horse.

Whilst the horse settled down to the challenge set him, the three in the cart he drew shared what space they had with sleeping-bags, food-boxes, writing-gear, Bibles

and books. And, of course, clothes. For these three were
Christian adventurers, bearers of Good News. All three
women of immense courage! 'There are demons in the
Gobi,' volunteered a guard outside a city gate. 'Must
you go?'

'Yes,' answered Mildred Cable, aware of what the
'Wall of Spears' could mean, 'I must go, because I am
seeking the lost—and some of them are out there!' And
with that, the great grinding wheels passed on. Did they
not know fear? Yes; but beyond that, they believed that
the God of Good News was with them.

The Gobi they found to be like an ocean bed—very
ancient, flat in places, stony, with petrified shells. In
parts its long mounds suggested the swell of great waves.
And there were the hilly parts, beloved of brigands! In
that land where time counted for nothing, they lay in
wait for passing caravans. Only where an occasional
spring showed itself as an oasis, was there life—a few
families. To keep the water-hole from being choked, and
to provide a *serai*—a bare enclosure, walled, for the
safety of tired travellers—served as justification for life
to them. Trains of camels came that way—the first with
a bell swinging at its neck; and other carts much like
their own, and rough caravans. They travelled in convoy
where possible, for safety, some fully armed, drawn by
tough little donkeys. Such adventurers might be carpet-
traders, merchants seeking jade, explorers, or collectors
of dinosaur eggs and other prehistoric finds for the
world's museums.

But because there were men and women and children
in such arid, dangerous places, the three gentle ladies
counted it their Christian duty to make their uncom-
fortable journeys. And *five times* they set out—each
gathering fresh hair-raising experiences—till it seemed
that they had done what they might, distributing Bibles,
carrying Good News of the Kingdom everlasting. *And
still many wait to hear!*

MY PRAYER

O God of truth and love, I marvel that you have spoken
to men and women since the beginning of time—
    through the words of your prophets;
    the poems of your psalmists;
    the stories of your gospel scribes.
I marvel that still today there are those who hazard their
lives to share this Good News—
    travellers, preachers and story-tellers;
    translators and commentators;
    scholars, and modern saints.
I bless you for the great Bible societies of the world,
which make the Bible available, today—
    in every tongue, at low cost, and in every place;
    through bookshops and colporteurs;
    by way of countless donators and collectors. A M E N

OUR PRAYER TOGETHER

O God of adventurers—Abraham, Peter, Paul, Aquila,
Priscilla, and countless others—
    we bless you that roads and trackless ways invite;
    we bless you for those who lift eyes to the far
      horizons;
    we bless you for those who today give themselves
utterly to the service of Christ.
Deliver us at home from judging the worthwhileness of
any undertaking merely in terms of monetary reward,
    in terms of publicity, popularity, excitement—
    and make us mindful of adventures of other kinds
      near at hand.
Direct our witness wherever we can make it, that fewer
may walk in darkness, in doubt, in fear.
    Let the beauty of the Lord our God be upon us;
    let the strong loveliness of Christ be in us;
    let the unchanging power of his Spirit support us.
    Now, and always. A M E N

FEI-YEN IN ACTION

Fei-Yen's eyes danced—she was overjoyed at the news that a school was to be opened near her village. She had so much wanted to read and write. War had been going on for over a year; though the local farmers were certain that it would never reach them. But how wrong they were!

The ominous sound of machine-gun fire was followed by a stream of refugees passing their way. Fei-Yen's father was shocked by the treatment some of the soldiers meted out to the women and girls. Some, who tried to save them, were roughly bayoneted. 'You must plan for yourself', he said. And Fei-Yen did. She made her way to a little clinic miles off, run by two Chinese under an overseas doctor. They were glad of any help.

A few weeks later, the enemy neared the little clinic. 'You must plan for yourself,' said the doctor—and once again, she did. It might not have surprised anyone, had she jumped in the well. Instead, she cut off her long hair, put on man's clothing, and farmer's boots. And so rigged, she returned. Unrecognized, she asked for a coolie's job. But so handy was she with the patients, that it dawned upon those concerned, who she was. They said nothing—they needed help so badly.

All day long, and into the night, the 'young coolie' worked among those brought into the little clinic— washed wounds, and bandaged limbs. The enemy were soon bringing in their own wounded—holding a pistol at the head of each clinic worker involved, lest their own men should lack anything. There was no danger that such would happen—though there was danger of another kind. When darkness allowed fellow-Chinese to stir, one clinic worker asked, 'What will they say if they discover that we have helped the enemy?' 'Kill us!' came the realistic reply. 'In any case,' suggested the young coolie, almost dropping with tiredness, 'let us sleep now, while we can.'

But in no time, a heavy knock on their door wakened them abruptly. And by lantern-light they opened it, to face whoever waited. It was, this time, a bedraggled company of their own Chinese fighting-men, with wounded. 'Come in!' uttered sleep-drowned Fei-Yen. And on through the rest of that night they toiled to help them.

A Sunday morning came, when the doctor of a hospital fifteen miles off was ready to conduct morning worship. He looked up to see a strange little coolie in the congregation—and not, as was usual, with the men on the right, nor on the left with the women. He sent someone to this little stranger in the passage. When a teacher later volunteered a name, the answer of the staff was: 'But if she's working, as you say, in the enemy area fifteen miles off, how did she get here, and why?' The answer from yet another possessed of the facts, was, 'They have run out of chloroform and anti-tetanus over there. And things are bad. So she came alone under cover of darkness, and climbed over our wall to get some.'

They had some idea what that meant, and one word was immediately on all lips—that one word was, 'Courage'.

There was no question about it. The little clinic where Fei-Yen found herself in disguise, was very hard-pressed —captured and re-captured time and again! She found words to make one prayer—and she prayed it constantly: '*O Lord, help us to root out of our hearts all pride, all anger, all fear . . . all that makes war!*'

MY PRAYER
I marvel that amidst the evil growth of war, good grows—
    courage blossoms in unexpected places;
    and the fruit of compassion is plucked.

I marvel that after so many centuries, nations still attempt
>   to settle their disputes in this way;
>   to pay the price of promising young lives.

I marvel that so much material wealth of the nations
>   is poured out so wastefully,
>   unjustly and hurtfully.

O God, let us, statesmen, ordinary citizens, refugees,
>   put our best brains and our hardly strained resources to new and peaceful purposes.

Foster within us, in every way, an out-reach of goodwill—
>   through travel, thoughtful reading, and
>   exchange of students.

Let us live to see a new day dawn. In the spirit of the Prince of Peace, our Lord. AMEN

OUR PRAYER TOGETHER

O God, make us 'instruments of your peace' today—
>   in our homes, and schools, and places of business;
>   in our churches and clubs, where standards are set;
>   in our council offices, and national governments.

Grant that those devoted to breaking down may be thwarted;
>   that more and more may desire to build up;
>   that national pride may be cleansed;
>   and the free breath of justice be known.

Give to all in situations of war and revolt, a new spirit,
>   that a day may come when peace-making is more exciting;
>   when, with war out-moded, we shall go forth into each day
>   without fear, and return to our homes at night without hurt.

Strengthen in all the earth, O God, the on-going ministry of the United Nations, and all who serve you there.

AMEN

GOD'S PEANUT MAN

It was a January evening in 1943—and the newsboys were calling, 'God's Peanut Man dead!' And some of us travelling in the flow of traffic, put down a few coins for a paper.

Plundering and burning had been the earliest things he remembered; men in the doorway of their cabin, and the sound of galloping hoofs. And the little Negro family was never together again. After a time, the raiders had made a deal—a horse, in exchange for the little bundle of supple arms and legs. The little boy soon showed he had a way with growing things. He scratched away at the surface of the earth. 'What is rain?' was one of his early questions. 'Who makes it?' And of flowers of all colours, 'Who brings them out of the same kind of earth?' His little mind always busy, he was soon big enough to make his way down the cornfield rows, carrying a load of seed—dropping it, two steps, three grains, two steps, three grains!

Somebody told little George Washington Carver that God made the world. There were so many things to learn —the ways of plants and flowers, living things. But it was desperately hard to get an education. There was a verse in the Bible that held him: of God, the Creator of all these wonderful things, it said: *'In all thy ways acknowledge him, and he shall direct thy paths'* (Proverbs 3:6).

Through all his growing up, it was his deepest longing to have a little bit of soil of his own. And by the time he reached twenty-three, that was realized—he owned a little bit in Kansas. At last he was a farmer. But that was not enough. Next, he wanted to be a university man —to be able to uncover some of the deep secrets hid in the earth. Since he had no family to support him, and no money, the only way was to earn by doing fellow-students' washing between studies.

But by the time the young enthusiast for growing things had his degree as a botanist, he had made it plain that a young man with a black skin could have as bright a brain as any. So well had he qualified, that he was asked to join the staff of the famous Tuskegee Agricultural Institute.

Soon, during a worrying time for many farmers growing cotton—owing to a serious boll-weevil attack—he was able to come forward with a suggested alternative crop. 'Why not grow peanuts?' Ridicule was all that was forthcoming from some—but not for long. George Carver, it was soon plain, was a man of deep knowledge, as well as of dependence on the Creator of all life's growing things. 'I told God,' said he humbly, at that time, 'that I wanted to know all about the peanut. And he gave me a handful of them to carry into my laboratory for thought. I set them out, I separated all their parts.'

In time, he was able to do for those dependent on such a lead, what had never before been attempted—to develop flour, butter, cheese from the peanut. Added to these commodities of every day, he developed also glycerine, soap, coffee, and medicines of several kinds—altogether, before death claimed him that day in 1943, *over three hundred products*!

Science faculties, and learned societies clamoured to give him honours; but to be modestly acknowledged as 'God's peanut man' seemed to Dr George Washington Carver the greatest honour of all! He and God worked together! All the world over now, many of us benefit from his devotion.

MY PRAYER

O God, I am amazed at what I know of this wonderful world you have made—

with its darkness surrendering to light;
with its colour and shape and creative surprise;

with earth's fertility matched to human need.
that they take nothing for granted;
I marvel at the questing minds of men, your partners—
that they are prepared for endless research;
that they are ready to share their finds with us all.
I accept my humble place as a steward of your good
gifts, too:
use what skills I have, to grow, and tend, and share;
use my joy in the greenness of the grass, the strength
of the trees;
use my harvest grains of fruit and corn, to meet
the needs of others besides myself.
Let me not fail you in my small share of your great
creation. For Christ's sake. A M E N

OUR PRAYER TOGETHER
O God, our Father, you waken us each morning to live
in your world—
fascinated by the rolling back of the darkness;
fascinated by the stirring of life around us;
fascinated by the discovery of fresh secrets.
We would not use your world alone for selfish ends—
show us how we can share with near and far;
guide amidst much confusion, men and women of
science;
support within fierce competition, all devoted to
commerce.
And save us all, O Lord, from selfish greed
that misuses and wastes the earth's resources;
that thinks only of its own ends;
that reckons only in money-columns.
Bless especially those who await from us a better understanding of those affairs of your family—if they are to
be fed.
Bless all young people serving through volunteer service
abroad. In the name of Christ. A M E N

MORE THAN WEEKENDS

David Sheppard's first games of cricket were played in Sussex. He was only a little fellow of eight then. His father—a London solicitor—had a weekend cottage in the village of Slinfold. Looking back, long after his father's early death, young David was to remember his score of 'twenty-three against the Veterans' XI' one of those weekends.

But life is more than weekends—and soon David's love of cricket was to embrace his whole life. For a little while—like many another school-boy of ten—his passion was planes and warships. Even though war had broken out—to be something more far-reaching than his game—he was still to enjoy his mother's unpredictable under-arm bowls. David's sister rather despised anything short of a fast round-arm, though every other delivery was likely to land in a prickly hedge.

Boarding-school at Bognor; then a sudden change of site, to avoid enemy bombing, brought cricket again to the fore. Then came Sherborne School, and a first match for the First XI. David was seventeen now, and young enough to remember forever that he 'was out for a duck'.

The later match at Hastings—when he made fifty—was a better memory to carry forward. Still at Sherborne, he played at Lord's for the first time—in a match between Southern Schools and The Rest—his captain on that memorable occasion, one later to become his cricket-test hero, Peter May. And that marked the passing of the school-boy, tall, gangly, enthusiastic.

Soon, he was off to barracks near Belfast, to do his two years' National Service in the Army. Life was becoming more serious—but there was still room for cricket. A bad run of dropped catches drove home the simple fact that he needed more practice, and more con-

fidence, if what a London paper was presently to call
'Sheppard's happy day' was to come—as it did come!

Whilst still at Sherborne, David had won an exhibition
to Trinity Hall, Cambridge. With a secret dream of becoming a barrister—influenced by early love for his
father, no doubt—he planned to spend two years reading history and the third in law. He could not know that
things were not to be that way—any more than, for him,
cricket could be reserved for recreation. *Life is more
than weekends*! A visiting preacher arrived to conduct a
mission in Cambridge—and, brought to the cross-roads
of choice, David became a Christian. He had held for
some time ideas about worship and morality—but this
was more. Parting from an undergraduate who had
given him help, as he was to write later, 'I walked back
to my room in Trinity Hall late that night . . . I knelt in
my bedroom and, praying in my own words, I asked
Christ to come into my life. . . . Then I prayed something like this: "Lord, I don't know where this is going
to take me, but I'm willing to go with you."'

And where has it taken him? Of a partial answer we
can be sure—to play cricket for England; to make 129,
and see that newspaper headline at last; to find himself
at Ridley Hall facing a theological training; to find himself, by 1955, not a barrister, but ordained to the Christian ministry by the Bishop of London in St Paul's; married; moving into ministry at the famous Mayflower
Family Centre in London's Canning Town; and now
to another 'happy day'—larger in its consequences than
a cricket score—to consecration as a youthful bishop.
This, just now, is 'where the action is'. And, more meaningful, amidst whatever the years must be left to uncover, is one fact: *'Faith is more than weekends!'*

MY PRAYER

O God, a lot of things keep on happening. But no part of
life finds me outside the scope of your interest—
    your love, your moulding pressures;

Also available in the Fontana Religious Series

The Plain Man Looks at the Lord's Prayer
WILLIAM BARCLAY
The historical background to and the precise meaning of the Lord's Prayer.

The Plain Man's Book of Prayers
WILLIAM BARCLAY
Written especially for Fontana by a distinguished scholar and gifted preacher to help those who wish to pray.

More Prayers for the Plain Man
WILLIAM BARCLAY
An essential companion to *The Plain Man's Book of Prayers*, containing slightly longer daily prayers and Bible readings.

The Mind of St Paul
WILLIAM BARCLAY
'A lucid exposition of many aspects of St Paul's thought.'
Church Quarterly

The Plain Man Looks at Himself
WILLIAM PURCELL
A book of self-examination for the ordinary Christian.

The Plain Man Looks at the Bible
WILLIAM NEIL
'A good popular guide book to the Bible which is well worth reading for its own sake.' *Church Times*

The Young Church in Action
J. B. PHILLIPS
Luke's work rendered into contemporary English.

Also available in the Fontana Religious Series

Prayers for Help and Healing
WILLIAM BARCLAY

William Barclay's books of prayers have now sold over 400,000 copies in Fontana. Here are prayers to help share private suffering of mind and body with God.

Letters to a Friend 1950–52
ROSE MACAULAY

Reveals her as one of the great letter-writers of this century. 'The book tingles with wit and blossoms with erudition and experience.' *Sunday Telegraph*

The General Next to God
RICHARD COLLIER

The story of William Booth, pawnbroker turned preacher, who founded the Salvation Army in the face of armed mobs, burned meeting halls and biased courts.

Half-way to Faith
DAVID ECCLES

'Lord Eccles writes with a charm and humility which hold the reader, and with a perception which should help both believer and non-believer to be asking the right questions.' *Archbishop of Canterbury, Sunday Times*

The Future of Man
TEILHARD DE CHARDIN

A giant footnote on his famous book *The Phenomenon of Man*. Teilhard here considers the future of mankind at three levels: science, philosophy and theology. 'It should be read by all who seek purpose in the universe.' *John Stuart Collis, Sunday Times*

Also available in the Fontana Religious Series

Good News For Modern Man
The New Testament—Today's English Version
Already known to 14 million people this translation has swept
America. Read by all denominations. Combines scrupulous
accuracy with the freshness and urgency of the Christian
message.

Life Line
ALAN WALKER
Alan Walker founded Life Line in Sydney to combat suicide
and help all in need. With its discipline, its efficiency, its
unique round-the-clock telephone counselling and its crash
rescue teams, Life Line shows Christianity in action.

A Woman's Book of Prayers
RITA F. SNOWDEN
'It seems to me to answer almost perfectly to its title. The
language is modern and yet beautiful. I am quite sure that
this book will make prayer more real and meaningful for all
who use it.' *William Barclay*

But That I Can't Believe
JOHN A. T. ROBINSON
Gives the lie to those who say the author of *Honest to God* and
The New Reformation, the man who started the great break-
through in radical theology in Britain, does not speak to the
man in the pew. Warm, lucid explanations of the joys and
doubts of the Christian faith, in down-to-earth language
everyone can understand.

Truth to Tell
HUGH MONTEFIORE
Cambridge sermons which take a pretty sharp look at
Christian faith and Christian ethics today, and suggest
some radical restatements.